THE POWERS THAT BE

STUDIES IN BIBLICAL THEOLOGY

THE
POWERS THAT BE

*Earthly Rulers and Demonic Powers
in Romans 13.1–7*

CLINTON MORRISON

WIPF & STOCK · Eugene, Oregon

To My Parents

Wipf and Stock Publishers
199 W 8th Ave, Suite 3
Eugene, OR 97401

The Powers That Be
By Morrison, Clinton D.
Copyright©1960 SCM Press
ISBN 13: 978-1-60899-025-2
Publication date 9/17/2009
Previously published by SCM Press, 1960

Copyright © SCM Press 1960
First English edition 1960 by SCM Press
This Edition published by arrangement with SCM-Canterbury Press

CONTENTS

Preface   8

Abbreviations   9

Introduction: An old problem and a new solution   11
    The problem   11
    A new solution is proposed   13
    The plan of Part One of this essay   14

PART ONE: A HISTORY AND EVALUATION OF RECENT INTERPRETATION OF ROMANS 13.1-7

I A POSITIVE CONTRIBUTION   17

The Jewish background of Paul's view of the spirit world   17
    Paul's basic frame of reference   17
    The spirit world of Judaism   18

Paul's use of an old concept   21
    The place of the angelic powers in early Christian thought   21
    The place of the spirit world in Paul's view of the State   22
    I Corinthians 2.6 ff.   23
    I Corinthians 6.1 ff.   24

Romans 13.1-7   25
    The linguistic argument   25
    The psychological argument   27
    The theological argument   28
        1. The theological context of the proposed exegesis   28
        2. The State in redemptive history: Christ and the powers   29
            a. The Christ-event and the present period   30
            b. Servants in the Kingdom of Christ   32
            c. The rule and servants of Christ in the light of eschatology   34
            d. The context of creation   35
        3. The State in early Christian thought: a summary   36

Contents

II	THE NEGATIVE REACTION	40
	Criticism of the new thesis on linguistic grounds	41
	Criticism on exegetical grounds	44
	Criticism on historical grounds	49
	Criticism on dogmatic grounds	51
III	AN EVALUATION AND PROSPECT	55
	The common ground of agreement	55
	Unresolved differences	56
	1. Linguistic	57
	2. Historical	58
	3. Exegetical	59
	4. Theological	61

PART TWO: AN EXEGETICAL CONTRIBUTION TO THE INTERPRETATION OF ROMANS 13.1–7

IV	TO THE ROMANS	63
	Communication and exegesis	63
	The Graeco-Roman conception of the State in the Cosmos	68
	The State and the Hellenistic spirit	69
	The background of the Graeco-Roman concept of the State in the Cosmos	70
	The Near Eastern background	70
	The Greek background	73
	Main currents in the Graeco-Roman period	75
	Power in the Graeco-Roman period	75
	Astrology in the Graeco-Roman period	77
	Monotheism in the Graeco-Roman period	80
	The concept of *daimones* in the Graeco-Roman period	83
	The divinity of the emperor	90
	Hellenistic Judaism	93
	The writer and the readers of the epistle	100
V	THE POWERS THAT BE	102
	The point of departure and the concluding problem	102
	Romans 13.1–7	104
	Introductory questions	104
	What Paul was 'imparting'	106

Contents

Elements in communication	109
1. 'The governing authorities' (*exousiai*)	109
2. The appointed servants and ministers	111
3. 'By God'	112
4. 'Be subject'	113
The theological context of the communication	114
Christ and the *exousiai*	114
The Christian and the *exousiai*	122
1. Christian subjection as relationship in faith	123
2. Subjection for conscience' sake	124
3. Christian freedom from the *exousiai*	127
Epilogue	130
Appendix A: CONCERNING THE RULER-CULT	131
Oriental and Greek aspects	131
'Deification' of the ruler	132
The fanatics	133
Qualifications	133
Titles and *proskynesis*	134
Appendix B: BIBLIOGRAPHY TO THE QUESTION OF JEWS IN ROME IN THE GRAECO-ROMAN PERIOD	137
Appendix C: SOME NEGATIVE CONSEQUENCES	138
Index of authors	140
Index of biblical references	142

PREFACE

The following essay is based upon my study in the summers of 1953–1955. In preparing the manuscript for publication, a number of more recent studies of importance to our discussion have been taken into account. Only the bibliography on the exegetical discussion of Rom. 13.1–7 is anywhere near complete; there is no end to the theological discussion of 'Church and State', or to the scholarly literature on Paul, late Judaism, and the Graeco-Roman period.

The conclusions to which I have come might have been reached in a number of other ways, based upon the study of different aspects of Paul's thought and other aspects of late antiquity. This essay is only one way, but it is also a new direction in the history of the problem it treats.

I wish to express my thanks and indebtedness to Dean Floyd V. Filson for his reading of my manuscript at various stages of writing, his friendly criticism and encouragement. Professor Oscar Cullmann has shown me many kindnesses associated with this work. My indebtedness to him as a scholar will be obvious, but it is no less a debt to him as a teacher whose first concern is to further research, not to build a 'school'. Thanks also are due to Professors Bo Reicke, C. F. D. Moule, and G. Ernest Wright for their reading of the manuscript and helpful comments. I wish to acknowledge the courtesy and carefulness of the SCM Press editorial staff and of Mr Donald L. Pannabecker, who helped me with the proofs. The shortcomings, however, are all my own.

McCormick Theological Seminary CLINTON MORRISON (jr.)
Chicago

ABBREVIATIONS

Bousset-G: W. Bousset, *Die Religion des Judentums im spathellenistischen Zeitalter*,[3] ed. H. Gressmann, Tübingen, 1926
BMC: *Coins of the Roman Empire in the British Museum*, I–V, 1923–50
CAH: *Cambridge Ancient History*
CD: Karl Barth, *Church Dogmatics*, ET, Edinburgh, 1936 ff.
Charles: R. H. Charles, *Apocrypha and Pseudepigrapha of the OT*, Oxford, 1913
CH: *Corpus Hermeticum*
ERE: *Encyclopaedia of Religion and Ethics*
ET: English translation
EvTh: *Evangelische Theologie*
Ginsberg: L. Ginsberg, *Legends of the Jews*, Philadelphia, 1910–38
Hennecke: E. Hennecke, *Neutestamentliche Apokryphen*,[2] Tübingen, 1923/4
HTR: *Harvard Theological Review*
HUCA: *Hebrew Union College Annual*
IAAM: H. Frankfort et al., *The Intellectual Adventure of Ancient Man*, Chicago, 1946; Cambridge, 1947
JHS: *Journal of Hellenic Studies*
JNES: *Journal of Near Eastern Studies*
Kautsch: E. Kautsch, *Apokryphen und Pseudepigraphen des AT*, Tübingen, 1900
KD: Karl Barth, *Kirchliche Dogmatik*, Munich and Zurich, 1932 ff.
KrS: *Kirchenblatt für die reformierte Schweiz*
Liddell-S: Liddell and Scott, *Greek-English Lexicon*, new (9th) ed., Oxford, 1925–40
LCL: *Loeb Classical Library*
Moore: G. F. Moore, *Judaism in the First Centuries of the Christian Era*, Cambridge, Mass., 1927–30
Moulton-M: J. H. Moulton and G. Milligan, *Vocabulary of the Greek NT*, London, 1914–29

Abbreviations

Nock-F: *Hermès Trismégiste*, ed. A. D. Nock, tr. A. M. J. Festugière (Collection Budé), Paris, 1945; notes by C(umont), E(inarson), F(estugière), N(ock) and R(euch)

Pauly-W: Pauly-Wissowa, *Realencyclopadie der klassischen Altertumswissenschaften*

PGM: K. Preisendanz, *Papyri Graecae Magicae*, Leipzig and Berlin, 1928–31

RAC: *Reallexikon für Antike und Christentum*

RGG: *Religion in Geschichte und Gegenwart*

SAH: *Sitzungsberichte der Heidelberger Akademie der Wissenschaften, philosophische-historische Klasse*

SBT: Studies in Biblical Theology

Schürer: E. Schürer, *History of the Jewish People in the Time of Jesus Christ*, ET, Edinburgh, 1885–91

Scott: W. Scott, *Hermetica*, Oxford, 1924–36

Strack-B: H. L. Strack and P. Billerbeck, *Kommentar zum NT aus Talmud und Midrasch*, Munich, 1922–8

TB: *Theologische Blätter*

TLZ: *Theologische Literaturzeitung*

TWNT: *Theologisches Wörterbuch zum NT*, Stuttgart, 1932 ff

TZ: *Theologische Zeitschrift*

ZNW: *Zeitschrift für die NT Wissenschaft*

Note: Bibliographies are given for each chapter, but do not include reference works, commentaries or ancient sources.

Numbers enclosed in parentheses refer to lines in reference works.

INTRODUCTION

AN OLD PROBLEM AND A NEW SOLUTION

The problem. The importance and complexity of Paul's words to the Romans concerning the State are well known in the history of the Church. The problem of the meaning of Christian freedom, civil responsibility, and divine authority in regard to the actual, ever changing circumstances of daily life makes an understanding of the New Testament's most direct statement on this matter a perpetual imperative. To the critical reader the question arises: How could Paul, when confronted with the actual situation in which the early Church found itself with regard to the State, express such an affirmative opinion concerning the governing authorities with such unshaken conviction and unconditional certitude?[1] Whether we begin at the beginning of the New Testament with John the Baptist, or at the core of it with Jesus Christ, or at the point of its formation in the life of the early Church, we find conflict with the State within the experience of Christianity from its inception.[2] The supreme lordship of Christ[3] and the unique character of membership in the Church[4] implied a way of life which did not conform to that of the world.[5] As Christian

BASIC BIBLIOGRAPHY: Gerhard BAUER, 'Zur Auslegung und Anwendung von Römer 13.1-7 bei Karl Barth', *Antwort*, Karl Barth zum 70. Geburtstag, ed. E. Wolf, Zollikon-Zürich, 1956, pp. 114-23. Gunther DEHN, 'Engel und Obrigkeit', *Theologische Aufsätze*, Karl Barth zum 50. Geburtstag, ed. E. Wolf, Munich, 1936, pp. 90-109. Martin DIBELIUS, *Die Geisterwelt im Glauben des Paulus*, Göttingen, 1909. Walter KÜNNETH, *Politik zwischen Dämon und Gott*, Berlin, 1954. H. SCHLIER, 'Die Beurteilung des Staates im Neuen Testament', *Zwischen den Zeiten* 10, 1932, 312-30. K. L. SCHMIDT, 'Das Gegenüber von Kirche und Staat in der Gemeinde des Neuen Testaments', *TB* 16, 1937, 1-16.

[1] Dehn, p. 90. Cf. Künneth, pp. 38 f.
[2] Mark 6.14 ff.; Luke 2.1; 23.2; John 19.12; Acts 17.6 f.; 24.5; (4.1).
[3] Mark 15.2; Acts 2.33, 36; 5.31; Phil. 2.9; Eph. 1.21; Heb. 12.2; 1.3 f.; Rom. 10.9, etc.
[4] Gal. 4.26; Eph. 2.19; Phil. 3.20; Col. 3.1 f.; Heb. 11.10, 13; 12.22; 13.14; I Peter 1.1; 2.11; Polycarp, *Phil.* 1.1; *I Clem.* 1.1.
[5] Mark 10.42 f.; 12.17; Acts 4.19; 5.29 (cf. Dan. 3.18); Rom. 6.12 f.; 12.2; Gal. 2.20; Eph. 4.22 f.; I Peter 1.14. Cf. Adolf Deissmann, *Light from the Ancient East*, ET, rev. ed., London, 1927, pp. 355 ff.; Schmidt, *passim*.

freedom was subject to misinterpretation and excess,[1] not only slaves[2] required special teaching, but all Christians needed to learn what their freedom meant in relationship to the State.[3] In this context Paul wrote to Rome and in this context his uncompromising words must be understood.

Outstanding among the problems of this passage is the fact that it is not easily harmonized with the views of other New Testament writers. While Paul designated the Roman authorities as 'servants of God' (Rom. 13.4), the writer of the Apocalypse identified the Roman state as the 'beast rising out of the sea'.[4] This inconsistency is complicated by the fact that in other passages Paul himself seems less disposed to commend the State. Far from calling the civil magistrates 'ministers of God' (Rom. 13.6), he designates them as those 'who are least esteemed by the church' (I Cor. 6.4).[5]

The traditional solution to Paul's conflicting statements regarding the State has been psychological: the spirit in which he wrote was tempered by his past experiences with civil government. Most commentators are careful to mention that the letter to the Romans was written in the earlier part of Nero's rule, before he persecuted the Christians. On more than one occasion Paul had received the protection of Roman justice (Acts 18.12 ff.; 19.38 ff.). Because his experience with civil authority had been favourable up to the time he wrote to Rome, it has been concluded that he felt no need to qualify his statement that the State was the 'servant of God'. It was only later that the demonic 'beast-like' character of the State became clear and the experience of persecution became the basis for negative evaluation of worldly authority.[6]

This effort to solve the inconsistencies in the New Testament's

---

[1] I Cor. 8.9; Gal. 5.13; I Peter 2.16.
[2] Eph. 6.5 ff.; Col. 3.22 ff.; I Tim. 6.1 f.; Titus 2.9 f.; I Peter 2.18.
[3] Rom. 13.1–7; I Peter 2.13–17; Titus 3.1; Dehn, pp. 92–94. Cf. Schlier, pp. 318 ff.
[4] Rev. 13.1, cf. v. 7. Schmidt (p. 9) cites other points of conflict in the NT: I Peter 2.13 ff., like Rom. 13, exhorts Christians to honour the State, while 5.13 refers to Rome as Babylon. Cf. also Luke 20.25 and 13.32; Schlier, pp. 329 f.; Künneth, pp. 41–43.
[5] Cf. Lukas Vischer, *Die Auslegungsgeschichte von I Kor. 6.1–11*, Tübingen, 1955, pp. 13 f.
[6] Schmidt, pp. 8 f.; Dehn, p. 94.

Introduction

evaluation of the State has been unsatisfactory to many because, as a matter of fact, Paul's experience with civil magistrates before he wrote Romans had not always shown them to be the best or most honourable of their kind. He had known human authorities who could not lightly be called 'servants of God'.[1] Furthermore, the passage in Paul's writings which appears most clearly to qualify, if not contradict, his statement to the Romans, i.e. I Cor. 6.1 ff., was written earlier than the great affirmative appraisal of civil authority. Whatever led Paul to refer to the magistracy as those 'least esteemed by the church', it was already known to the author of Romans. In addition to this, the psychological analysis fails to account for the fact that the view of I Peter (2.13 ff.), which is similar to that of Romans 13, was held in a time of persecution.[2] In short, Paul's view of the State as the servant of God cannot be attributed to a distillation of his personal experience.

In like manner the various efforts to interpret the Romans passage as an abstract statement of what the State *ought* to be, quite apart from the question of whether or not Paul had ever found it to be so, have been unconvincing. Attempts to provide a solution from the history of other religions have never been too successful in showing Paul's dependence upon the apparently parallel views.

A new solution is proposed. The inconclusive character of the traditional attempts to explain Paul's bold affirmation of the State in Romans 13, and its relationship to contradictory passages in the New Testament, led Gunther Dehn in 1936 to try a *theological* explanation.[3] Although theology furnished the impetus, it would be wrong to conclude that Dehn's contribution rested upon a purely theological foundation; the basic elements with which the first theological interpreters worked were formulated in clear terms more than two decades earlier through the scientific exegetical scholarship of Martin Dibelius.[4]

---

[1] Acts 16.20–24; Rom. 8.35 f.; I Cor. 4.9, 12; 15.30 f.; II Cor. 1.8 f.; 4.3–11; 6.4 f., 9; 7.5; 11.23 ff.; Phil. 1.30; I Thess. 2.2 (cf. Heb. 10.32 f.).

[2] Cf. I Tim. 2.1 f.; Titus 3.1. See further *Mart. Polycarp* 10.2; Polycarp, *Phil.* 12.3; Schmidt, p. 3.

[3] Dehn, p. 100. For a recent summary of ambiguities and problems in traditional exposition of this passage, and the steps leading to a theological interpretation, cf. G. Bauer, pp. 114–17.

[4] *Op. cit.* H. Schlier, 'Mächte und Gewalten im Neuen Testament', *TB* 9,

It is in keeping with the actual history of what appears to be a recent interpretation that our review will be based upon exegetical work which began with Dibelius. From there we will move on to the theological interpretation which was fully developed by Barth and Cullmann. To begin with Dibelius' basic work means that we begin, not at all in a concern with the problem of the Christian's relationship to the State, but with the apparently remote discussion of the significance of the spirit world in Paul's writings. The development of the new interpretation from such a beginning was neither accidental nor artificial. The relationship between the spirit world and the State, which led the earlier interpreters to a bold conclusion, has proved to be the proper basis of the fully developed thesis. It will be interesting to note, in the controversy to follow, that the strength of those who propose the new interpretation has been in looking at the problem from the perspective of the spirit world in Paul's thought, while others have criticized it from the standpoint of the 'historical' Christian idea of the State.

The plan of Part One of this essay. In *chapter I* an effort will be made to present without criticism the substance and point of view of the new interpretation. Although not all contributors to the development of the theological exegesis agree with the final result, nor are those who fully developed it without criticism for its earlier forms, the first chapter will strive to present the main line of development, noting the exceptions to it. *Chapter II* will try to present an account of the principal criticisms which have until now been brought to bear against the interpretation in chapter I. While in many ways the arguments of the first two chapters have been expanded for clarification, the writer has not included views or evidence which *could* have been brought to bear on the question but which as a matter of fact had no place in the history of the discussion. Likewise certain biblical and pseudepigraphical evidence is frequently added to give the context of a particular scholar's point, but the present writer has not supplied a complete exegesis of passages which received no such detailed treatment by the men whose views are being represented. It is hoped that this presentation of the first two chapters without criticism will

---

1930, also was of indirect support. In light of the new interpretation, however, Dibelius reversed his earlier judgment in 'Rom und die Christen im ersten Jahrhundert', *SAH* 1941/42, 2. Abhandlung (1942), p. 7 n. 2.

Introduction

enable the reader to enjoy something of the excitement of the original conflict over the interpretation. *It is in chapter III that the point of view of the present writer is first presented* in an evaluation of both the new interpretation and the criticisms of it. It is then that the task of the second part of this essay will be defined. While it perhaps would be formally more correct to begin with an 'uncontroversial' exegesis of Romans 13.1–7, this has been decided against because (*a*) the passage as traditionally interpreted is relatively free from subtleties and ambiguities, and a careful reading of the text is quite sufficient to enter into the discussion in chapter I, and (*b*) the meaning of the passage as a whole cannot be isolated from the main subject of this essay, and therefore an exposition is properly a concluding rather than introductory matter.

Part One

A HISTORY AND EVALUATION OF RECENT INTERPRETATION OF ROMANS 13.1-7

I

A POSITIVE CONTRIBUTION

THE JEWISH BACKGROUND OF PAUL'S VIEW OF THE SPIRIT WORLD

Paul's basic frame of reference. An exegetical concern with Paul's view of the spirit world must first begin with the environment of ideas which he shared. While he accepted the concepts of Jewish

BASIC BIBLIOGRAPHY: Karl BARTH, *Christengemeinde und Bürgergemeinde*, Zollikon-Zürich, 1946 (ET in *Against the Stream*, London, 1954, pp. 15-50); *Rechtfertigung und Recht*,[2] Zollikon-Zürich, 1944; 'Volkskirche, Freikirche, Bekenntniskirche', *EvTh* 3, 1936, 411-22. W. BIEDER, *Ekklesia und Polis im Neuen Testament und in der Alten Kirche*, Zürich, 1941. Rudolf BULTMANN, *Theology of the New Testament*, ET, 2 vols., London, 1952, 1955. Oscar CULLMANN, *Christ and Time*, ET, London, 1951; *Christology of the New Testament*, ET, London, 1959; *The Earliest Christian Confessions*, ET, London, 1949; *Königsherrschaft Christi und Kirche im Neuen Testament*,[2] Zollikon-Zürich, 1946; *The State in the New Testament*, London, 1957; 'Zur neuesten Diskussion über die ἐξουσίαι in Röm. 13.1', *TZ* 10, 1954, 321-36. G. DEHN, see p. 11. M. DIBELIUS, see p. 11. M. JONES, 'St Paul and the Angels', *The Expositor*, 8th Series, 15, 1918, 356-70, 412-25. W. KÜNNETH, see p. 11. G. H. C. MACGREGOR, 'Principalities and Powers: The Cosmic Background of St Paul's Thought', *New Testament Studies* 1, 1954, 17-28. W. MANSON, 'Principalities and Powers', *Studiorum Novi Testamenti Societas*, Bulletin 3, 1952, pp. 7-17. E. PETERSON, 'Das Problem des Nationalismus im alten Christendom', *TZ* 7, 1941, 81-91. B. REICKE, *Diakonie, Festfreude und Zelos in Verbindung mit der altchristlichen Agapenfeier*, Uppsala, 1951; *The Disobedient Spirits and Christian Baptism*, Copenhagen, 1946. H. SCHLIER, see p. 11 for 'Staates'; 'Mächte und Gewalten im Neuen Testament', *TB* 9, 1930, 289-97. K. L. SCHMIDT, see p. 11. Wolfgang SCHWEITZER, *Die Herrschaft Christi und der Staat im Neuen Testament*, Zürich, 1948. James S. STEWART, 'On a Neglected Emphasis in New Testament Theology', *Scottish Journal of Theology* 4, 1951, 292-301. W. A. VISSER 'T HOOFT, *The Kingship of Christ*, London, 1948. H.-D. WENDLAND, 'Die Weltherrschaft Christi und die zwei Reiche', *Kosmos und Ekklesia*, Festschrift für Wilhelm Stählin, Kassel, 1953, pp. 23-39.

apocalyptic[1] and while these ideas may help explain his words, Paul had no interest in the speculative logic, the detail and fancy, in which popular Judaism indulged. These concepts appear in his writings only within the context of his primary concern for the faith and life of the Church, and therefore, secondly, we must always consider the ideas of the ancient world from the same perspective as did Paul, a man in Christ.[2]

The spirit world of Judaism. In its general aspects the spirit world of Judaism was thought to consist of countless radiant beings which adorned the splendour and majesty about the divine throne. They lacked for the most part the personality of names or the individuality of volition.[3]

A favourite theme connected with the spirit world of Judaism was the conception of the heavenly court. This council of spiritual beings, known as *bene elohim* ('sons of God')[4] or *kedoshim* ('holy ones'),[5] was presided over by God. They formed the '*familia* on high'[6] with whom all divine decisions were discussed before God (alone) ordained what should come to pass in the earth below.[7]

The old oriental device of casting the events of heaven and earth in parallel[8] was particularly evident in regard to the interests of the heavenly council. The involvement of gods (in Judaism only angels) in earthly affairs made a noteworthy impression upon Jewish thought in the concept of guardian angels who were placed over the nations ('folk angels').[9] The best known Old Testament passages relating the peoples of the earth to the spirit world are Deut. 32.8 (LXX); Dan. 10.13, 20 f.; 12.1.

---

[1] Dibelius, p. 182. Cf. Bultmann, I, 188 f., 172 ff., and esp. II, 146 ff.; E. Hennecke, pp. 17* f.; Macgregor, p. 19.

[2] Bultmann, II, 146 f.

[3] For angelic beings *as such* Paul has hardly any thought. Cf. Gal. 1.8; 4.14; I Cor. 13.1; Dibelius, pp. 183 ff.; Moore, I, 410 f., III, 123 n. 130 (to I, 401 ff.); Ginsberg, VII, 30–38. (Cf. Karl Barth's survey of theological reflection on angels in *KD* III/3 §51, 1st part; Jones, p. 422.)

[4] Job 1.6; 2.1. *Bene elim*, Pss. 29.1; 89.7, etc. Moore, I, 402 n. 2; Bousset-G, p. 321 n. 1; Charles, II, 191, note to En. 6.2.

[5] Ps. 89.6, 8; Job 5.1; 15.15; Deut. 33.2; Zech. 14.5; (Amos 4.2, LXX); Moore, I, 402 n. 3; Bousset-G, p. 321 n. 2; Charles, II, 189, note to En. 1.9.

[6] Moore, I, 407; Strack-B, I, 741 ff.

[7] Dibelius, pp. 186 f.; Moore, I, 407.

[8] Cf. Strack-B, III, 818; Bousset-G, pp. 323 f.; Moore, I, 403 f. See below, pp. 70–73.

[9] Cf. Peterson, pp. 84 ff. on the possibility of Hellenistic origin.

A Positive Contribution

Deut. 32.8 is concerned with the occasion when mankind was divided into nations and Israel was chosen. The number of peoples was established according to the number of *bene elohim*, 'sons of God'.[1] Every people except Israel was given over to the guardianship of an angelic prince (i.e. heavenly counsellor), but Israel was kept for Yahweh's own.[2] The fortunes of each nation on earth varied as did that of its respective folk angel. As the concept of folk angels remained current into the later Roman period, we learn from the Midrashim that the angels which Jacob saw in his dream, ascending and descending the heavenly ladder, were the angelic princes of the peoples. The rising of one of these folk angels indicated that power and dominion was exercised by his people on earth, and his descending to be replaced by the angel of another people indicated that another world power had ascended to authority in the world below. Jacob saw the angels of Babylonia, Persia, Greece, and Edom (Rome) each ascending in turn. When he saw the angel of Rome rising without yet a sign of descending, he became fearful, but was comforted by God, who told him that Rome too would be cast down and that no foreign power would deprive Israel of his place at God's right hand.[3] This subjected place of Israel among the nations and under the ascendancy of their guardian angels was taken into account in En. 89.59f. The seventy shepherds (folk angels) were commissioned to pasture the sheep (Israel) and to destroy (executing divine vengeance) only as many as God commanded. The excessive suffering of Israel under the domination of foreign powers, especially the destruction of the righteous, was thus to be attributed to the disobedience of the folk angels who would be judged for their work.[4]

[1] RSV and modern versions with the LXX (*bene el*, cf. Bertholet, H. W. Robinson, Marti [3rd ed.], and [according to Driver] Cheyne, Cornill, Schultz, Stade). Cf. Dibelius, pp. 193 f.; Moore I, 226 ff.; Bousset-G, pp. 326, 502 ff.

[2] Ecclus. 17.17 and Jub. 15.30 ff. (see notes in Charles); cf. Deut. 4.19; 29.25 f.; Moore, I, 226; II, 242 n. 1; Bousset-G, pp. 324 f.; Strack-B, III, 48 ff., I, 741 ff.; Schmidt, p. 15; Lagrange's Semitic background to Rom. 13.

[3] Strack-B, III, 49; cf. Ginsberg, I, 351.

[4] En. 90.20 ff.; cf. Fichtner in Kleinknecht et al., 'ὀργή', *TWNT* V, 405 (6–10). All angelic creatures were agents of God's will, regardless of their own intentions, and through this viewpoint Judaism avoided dualism. Job. 1 f., II Sam. 24.16; cf. Rev. 13.5; Moore, I, 403 f., 407; III, 124 n. 138, (III, 123 nn. 131, 133); Strack-B, III, 412 f. On the judgment of folk angels, cf. Charles and Kautzsch, notes to En. 89.59 and Jub. 15.31. Cf. Pss. 58, 82;

The Powers That Be

It is in this context that the passages in Daniel (10.13, 20 f.; 12.1) find their meaning. The book is concerned with a period when Israel was suffering under foreign domination. The counterpart of this strife is portrayed in the heavenly places where Michael, who appears as Yahweh's champion on Israel's behalf, contends with the angel-princes of the dominant powers, first Persia, then Greece. It was in this heavenly contest that many Jews placed their hope for freedom from the great world rulers, not merely because they despaired of driving their powerful oppressors out of the land by physical might, but because a certain priority was attached to the events in the heavenly spheres. Tradition held that God would not judge a nation until he had first judged and punished its angel prince.[1]

In the Graeco-Roman period Jewish national hope was inseparable from their religious doctrine, and both were woven into the very fabric of the people's cosmology. The nations which ruled the ancient world and successively oppressed the Jews were believed to be under the supervision and authority of their respective guardian angels, who were constantly under the supreme power and rule of the Creator of heaven and earth. Israel was his people and they could trust that his will would be done on earth as in heaven.

As will be seen later, there are other concepts of diverse origin which supplement the idea of folk angels in the ancient belief in 'world rulers', the area where Jewish angelology made its deepest penetration into Pauline theology.[2] However diverse the origin of the elements of their cosmology, the Jews strongly subordinated them to the faith that they were Yahweh's people and he alone was Creator and Ruler of the world. Their political viewpoint was inseparable from the cosmological-eschatological framework of their nationalistic religious hope.

Isa. 24.21 ff.; Gunkel, *Einleitung in die Psalmen* (Göttingen, 1933), p. 365; Reicke, *Diakonie*, pp. 356 f.; *Spirits*, pp. 133 ff.; G. Ernest Wright, *The Old Testament Against its Environment* (SBT 2), 1950, pp. 30–41 (on Ps. 82); Otto Eissfeldt, 'Yahweh Zebaoth', *Miscellanea Academica Berolinensia*, Berlin, 1950, pp. 128–50; Frank M. Cross, Jr., 'The Council of Yahweh in Second Isaiah', *JNES* 12, 1953, 274–7.

[1] Cf. the literal order in Isa. 24.21 ff. To support this concept further, rabbinical exegesis displayed considerable ingenuity; cf. Strack-B, III, 49 ff.

[2] Dibelius, pp. 189, 192–7.

A Positive Contribution

PAUL'S USE OF AN OLD CONCEPT

The place of the angelic powers in early Christian thought. Although many good works on the history of religion have traced biblical concepts to extra-biblical sources, there has been a general failure to consider the degree to which the early Christians shared and experienced in their own lives the truth of concepts common to their age. This has been neglected because of the conviction that there actually are no such things as 'angelic powers'.[1] But these spirit beings, as indicated above, were actually thought to belong to the temporal order of the world; they came with its creation and would also go with its passing, but so long as the world order endured, the New Testament affirms that 'all these powers are nothing other than the representatives of the world, who rule it.'[2]

This observation means more than adding a footnote to the history of religions. Cullmann has made clear the unusual prominence given to the angelic powers in the religious understanding of the first Christians;[3] they 'are particularly mentioned in every place where (Christ's) complete Lordship is being discussed'.[4]

We must conclude from this fact that these powers, in the faith of primitive Christianity, did not belong merely to the framework 'conditioned by the contemporary situation'. It is these invisible beings who in some way—not, to be sure, as mediators, but rather as executive instruments of the reign of Christ—*stand behind what occurs in the world.*[5]

Schlier also is impressed by the strong personal reality of the concept of heavenly powers for the early Fathers, and he feels that a proper understanding of the place of these powers in patristic thought is essential to the understanding of early Christian belief.[6]

---

[1] Schlier, 'Mächte', p. 289; Stewart, pp. 292–301; Manson, pp. 8 f.
[2] Schlier, 'Mächte', p. 291. Cf. Schmidt, p. 11; Cullmann, *Time*, pp. 191 f.; Jones, p. 423.
[3] Cullmann, *Confessions* ch. 4, esp. pp. 58–62; 'Diskussion', pp. 326 f.
[4] Cullmann, *Time*, p. 191, cf. pp. 103, 153, 192 f.
[5] *Ibid.*, p. 192; cf. Macgregor, p. 17 and *passim*; Stewart, *passim*.
[6] Schlier, 'Mächte', p. 289; cf. Bultmann, II, 145. Tatian, *Address* 29 (and frequently, e.g. 8, 9, 14, 19). Justin, *Dial.* 41.1 (and frequently, e.g. 56, 127). Note also, in regard to later discussion (see p. 23 n. 2 below), Justin's belief in these angel-demonic beings as constituting the 'host' over which *Christ* is Lord (*ibid.*, 85, ref. Ps. 24.7). All things on earth were entrusted to angels (Justin, *II Apology* 5) and Jews were their instruments in persecuting

The Powers That Be

The place of the spirit world in Paul's view of the State. At this point we should limit the discussion to the field of our special concern: Is the manifold relationship between angels and princes, 'world rulers' and earthly empires, Satan and 'this world', which is so evident in Judaism, present to any degree in Paul's view of the spirit world and earthly rulers?

First of all it must be stated that nowhere in the New Testament is there an intentional exposition of the Jewish doctrine of folk angels. This, however, should not be at all surprising, for nowhere do we find Paul turning aside from his principal concern with the Christian faith and life to set forth Jewish doctrine. His calling was to 'preach Christ, and him crucified.' The absence of a full presentation of some particular concept common to his time is not a decisive argument against Paul's having shared it, particularly if there is scattered evidence to the effect that such a concept was understood, accepted, and in some way useful in what he felt called to proclaim clearly. The relationship between the civil authorities and the spirit powers, which has been shown to be common to Jewish thought of his time, is evident in several places in the New Testament.

The very vocabulary which designates these powers lends weight to the impression that Paul was aware of a correspondence between the spirit world and the State. The term 'lords' ($\kappa\acute{\upsilon}\rho\iota\text{o}\iota$) in I Cor. 8.5, for example, refers to angelic powers, but the same word could equally apply to the succession of earthly rulers in the Near East.[1] Dehn suggests (p. 103) that the passages which relate to the Law's being given through angels may indirectly refer to

---

Christians (*Dial.* 131, ref. Deut. 32.7 ff. LXX!). Justin makes significant use of the LXX text of Isa. 30.4, Job 1.6, Ps. 96.5 in *Dial.* 79. Cf. *I Clem.* 36, *Barn.* 12, Athenagoras, *Apol.* 24.

[1] Acts 25.26. Deissmann, *op. cit.*, p. 355. Cf. *Acts of John* 98, *Acts of Philip* 68, 136 (cited by Schlier, 'Mächte', p. 292); Schmidt (p. 15) feels the contemporary belief in the mediation of God's rule through angelic powers is well enough attested in this period to confirm the association of powers and State as an active concept in early Christian thought (cf. Reicke, *Spirits*, pp. 134 f.). Schmidt feels this is rendered decisive by the fact that, in the NT, deification of the State is nothing other than a false worship of angels (Col. 2.10; Heb. 1 f.); these are the same angels who crucified Christ (I Cor. 2.8). Reicke (*Diakonie*, pp. 355–8) demonstrates that the slander of the powers was indicative of anarchy.

A Positive Contribution

the old Jewish belief which identified the angels present on Mount Sinai with the angel princes of the peoples. According to this view the Law was pronounced in seventy languages, but every nation except Israel refused it.[1]

In the light of this general evidence, Paul's use of Ps. 110 takes on particular significance. While the 'enemies' mentioned in the psalm refer to the nations which oppressed Israel, Paul has applied the term in I Cor. 15.24 f. and Eph. 1.20 ff. to the heavenly powers. The same kind of association is evident in Paul's use of Isa. 45.23 in Phil. 2.10 f. That Paul has obviously applied to the heavenly powers passages which refer to nations offers evidence that he accepted a system in which there were angelic powers behind the things of this world, including the nations and their rulers. That Paul should associate the Old Testament's hope for Israel with the defeat of spiritual powers was only natural in the light of the contemporary belief that victory over earthly powers must be initiated in the heavenly spheres. The proclamation of Christ's exaltation to the right hand of God was a forceful declaration of his authority and power, not only in the heavenly places, but also over all the rulers and powers of earth. Polycarp follows Paul's thought, interpreting the resurrection of Christ in terms of his victory and lordship over the powers who are his servants.[2]

The most important passages in regard to Paul's knowledge and use of the idea of angelic powers behind the civil authorities are I Cor. 2.6 ff., 6.1 ff., and Rom. 13.1 ff.

I Cor. 2.6 ff.—Concerned with the 'wisdom' of the gospel over against the foolishness of the world's wisdom, Paul wrote that it was precisely because the 'rulers (ἄρχοντες) of this age' did not

---

[1]Gal. 3.19; Heb. 2.2; Acts 7.38, 53. See Strack-B, III, 554, cf. III, 48 ff.; Ginsberg, V, 204–6.

[2]*Phil.* 2.1. Cf. Justin's use of Ps. 110 to declare Christ's relationship to the 'demons' who are none other than 'the gods of the nations' (Ps. 95.5 (LXX); *Dial.* 83.1; 121.3). Christ was therefore identified as 'King of glory' and 'Lord of powers' who were also the motivating force behind kings (Ps. 23 (LXX); cf. *Dial.* 29.1; 36.2; 85.1, 4, 5; cf. p. 21 n. 6 above). In the LXX of the Psalms 'lord of powers' is used consistently to translate *Yahweh Sabaoth*. Cf. Cullmann, *Konigs.*, pp. 5 ff.; *Time*, pp. 153, 193. Charles (on Jub. 15.31) suggests I Cor. 10.19; Gal. 4.3, 9; Col. 2.20 in context with En. 89. 51 ff., 90.22; Dibelius, p. 187, sees the concept of the heavenly council behind Gal. 3.19 and I Cor. 4.9; Dehn, p. 106, considers the well known problem of II Thess. 2.7 in the context of this interpretation; cf. however Cullmann, *Time*, pp. 164 ff., and Reicke, *Diakonie*, p. 358.

know the wisdom of God that they crucified Jesus.¹ Dibelius believes it most unlikely 'that Paul, who always seeks the driving forces of redemptive history in the realm of spirits, should here refer to the human cause of Jesus' crucifixion.'² The rulers of this age are rather the angelic powers, lords over this world, the 'elemental spirits' (στοιχεῖα).³ Dehn observes that the newer exegesis which considers the rulers as purely spiritual powers is almost as defective as the older interpretation of them as merely earthly officials, for *this passage actually represents in itself an immediate coincidence of heavenly and earthly activity* when Pilate, the high priests, and others were effectively in the power of their spiritual superiors.⁴ So understood, this passage appears to be a clear case of Paul's reliance upon the form of Judaism's belief in folk angels.⁵

I Cor. 6.1 ff.—Faced with the problem of the Corinthians' seeming inability to settle their common everyday disputes without recourse to civil courts, Paul reminded them that Christians would judge the world and the angels. The mention of both Cosmos and angels in reference to the courts recalls the parallel between the two in Jewish thought, according to which everything on earth had its own angel in heaven and the angels governed the world.⁶ Here the figure of the civil magistrate is significantly at

[1] Dibelius, pp. 134 ff., 148. Cf. RSV margin to Col. 1.26.

[2] Dibelius, p. 90. Supporting Dibelius (after Everling and Klöpper) are Massie, Craig, Moffatt, Lietzmann, Schmiedel, Weiss, Bousset, cf. C. A. Scott, 'The Dualistic Element in the Thinking of St. Paul', *Expository Times* 23, 1911/12, p. 561; Jones, pp. 364, 416 f. The older view, by which Jewish and Roman officials are meant, is maintained (usually with knowledge of the above view) after Marcion, Origen, etc., by Goudge, Parry, Meyer (5th ed.), Plummer and Robertson ('the very perverse suggestion of Schmiedel. . . .'), Heinrici, Bachmann, Godet. O. Holtzmann cannot decide.

[3] Cf. Dibelius, p. 200; Bultmann, II, 147, 150, 152. Cf. Dibelius, pp. 88–99 for a detailed comparison with Asc. Is. 10.7–11.35; Delling, 'ἄρχων', *TWNT* I, 488 (2).

[4] Dehn, p. 104. Supporting this view are Cullmann, *Königs.*, p. 25, *Time*, pp. 191, 196; W. Schweitzer, p. 19, cf. p. 34; W. Meyer, Schlatter; Macgregor, pp. 22 f.; Stewart, pp. 295 f. Cullmann ('Diskussion', p. 331) uses to his advantage the fact that modern scholars are divided over the question; by acknowledging each side to have validity, he emphasizes his view that Paul spoke of both spiritual and earthly powers simultaneously.

[5] W. Schweitzer carries the parallelism even further: Christ himself was represented in the heavenly warfare by the archangel Michael (p. 22). Cf. Hennecke, p. 330.

[6] Dehn, p. 105. Cf. Strack-B, III, 51.

A Positive Contribution

the centre of the concern, and the implications are that Christians will not only judge earthly magistrates (the form of the State, and the world, in this instance), but also the angels behind them. The Jewish concept of folk angels is basic to Paul's thought here also, and, as he makes no explanation of it in either chapter 2 or 6, it may be assumed to be common knowledge in the Corinthian church.[1]

ROMANS 13.1–7

In Romans 13 Paul understood that behind the pagan government there were spiritual powers of the same sort that operated in the death of Jesus.[2] *The rule of the Roman Empire was the simultaneous integrated endeavour of spiritual and human authorities.*

The linguistic argument.—The evidence for such a statement is, first of all, linguistic.[3] In Pauline literature 'authorities' (ἐξουσίαι), including the singular used in such a way as to indicate a plurality, i.e. 'every authority')[4] is consistently used to refer to the spiritual powers.[5] It is significant that it is usually associated with similar

[1] Dibelius, pp. 7–13. Cf. Cullmann, *Time*, pp. 191 f., 193; *Königs.*, p. 25; Manson, pp. 7 f. This interpretation is supported directly by Massie, Findlay, Moffatt, and indirectly (in ref. to En. 90.24 f., etc.) by Bousset, Weiss. Schmiedel, Lietzmann, Wendland, and W. Meyer (cf. I, 83 and 202), are vague, while Godet, Meyer, and Robertson and Plummer oppose more than the simple meaning.

[2] I Cor. 2.8. Dibelius, p. 200. Supporting this view are K. L. Schmidt ('Zum theologischen Briefwechsel zwischen Karl Barth und Gerhard Kittel', *TB* 13,1934, pp. 328–34), who early made one of the clearest identifications: 'The earthly State, . . . whose power and worth are of course not to be disparaged when in their proper place, belongs, according to Romans 13, to the *exousiai*, i.e. to the angelic and demonic powers. This understood, the biblical theological concept of the State as the Beast from the abyss becomes intelligible,' p. 332; cf. Schmidt, pp. 11, 15; Dehn, pp. 100 f.; Barth, 'Volkskirche', p. 413 (cf. pp. 416, 420); *Recht*, p. 15; Cullmann, *Königs.*, pp. 25–27, 44–48; *Time*, pp. 191–210; 'Diskussion', *passim*; Schweitzer, p. 19; B. Reicke, 'Law and this World, according to Paul', *Journal of Biblical Literature* 70, 1951, p. 269 (and n. 34); *Spirits*, pp. 134 f.; *Diakonie*, pp. 352, 357; Bieder, pp. 28 f.; Robert Morgenthaler, 'Roma—Sedes Satanae. Röm. 13, 1 ff. im Lichte von Luk. 4, 5–8', *TZ* 12, 1956, p. 303; Künneth, pp. 40 f.; (cf. H.-D. Wendland, *passim*). Parry (commenting on Rom. 13.1) curiously cites I Cor. 15.24, Eph. 1.21, etc., but makes no conclusion.

[3] To the works in the previous note add Schlier, 'Staates', p. 323.

[4] It is important to make clear that this discussion relates only to the *plural*, as singular usage does not conform to the consistent pattern of the plural.

[5] Rom. 13.1; I Cor. 15.24; Eph. 1.21; 3.10; 6.12; Col. 1.16; 2.10, 15. (Titus 3.1; I Peter 3.22.) Cf. Eph. 2.2. The only other plural in the NT is in Luke 12.11, where civil authorities as such are intended.

The Powers That Be

words, e.g. with 'principalities' (ἀρχαί),[1] 'powers' (δυνάμεις),[2] 'dominions' (κυριότητες),[3] 'names' (ὀνόματα),[4] 'world rulers' (κοσμοκράτορες),[5] 'spiritual hosts' (πνευματικά),[6] 'thrones' (θρόνοι),[7] 'angels' (ἄγγελοι),[8] 'rulers' (ἄρχοντες).[9] With the exception of Rom. 8.38 every significant Pauline reference to the spiritual powers who exercise authority upon earth includes *exousiai*, and it seems to those who support the new interpretation that a different understanding of the word in Romans 13 has no authority from its use in Paul's writings.

From the record of Paul's use of *exousiai* it becomes apparent that its meaning must be considered along with those other words which make up the vocabulary designating the spiritual powers. It has long been obvious that this terminology is shared with the concept of earthly governmental authority,[10] and this has been explained variously, e.g. by saying that the ancients believed the spirit world to have an internal order similar to their own,[11] or that the heavenly rulers were thought to preside over earthly affairs much as their own earthly rulers governed.[12] But Paul's use of terminology seems to imply more than this and to be quite capable of embodying the Jewish concept of folk angels.[13] This means that there is more than analogy involved. There is a special close relationship between spiritual and earthly rulers, making their rule essentially one. Although uninterested in setting forth the Jewish

---

[1] I Cor. 15.24; Eph. 1.21; 3.10; 6.12; Col. 1.16; 2.10, 15. (Titus 3.1.)
[2] I Cor. 15.24; Eph. 1.21; (I Peter 3.22;) cf. Rom. 8.38.
[3] Eph. 1.21; Col. 1.16; cf. Reicke, *Diakonie*, pp. 355, 357 f., 361.
[4] Eph. 1.21 (cf. Phil. 2.9).
[5] Eph. 6.12.
[6] τῆς πονηρίας, Eph. 6.12.
[7] Col. 1.16.
[8] (I Peter 3.22).
[9] Cf. I Cor. 2.6, 8. Plural elsewhere in Paul only Rom. 13.3 (cf. Eph. 2.2).
[10] Schmidt, p. 11; 'Zum Briefwechsel', *op. cit.*, p. 332; Dehn, p. 110; Schweitzer, pp. 17 f.; Foerster, 'ἐξουσία', *TWNT* II, 562 (17 ff.).
[11] Schmidt, p. 11 n. 26; Bauer on ἀρχή (ET, Arndt and Gingrich, *Greek-English Lexicon of the NT*, Cambridge, 1957).
[12] Delling, 'ἀρχή', *TWNT* I, 481 (36 ff.), cf. p. 487 (2 ff.).
[13] *Angels*: von Rad, 'ἄγγελος', *TWNT* I, 76 f.; Kittel, *ibid.*, I, 85 (10 ff.). *Principalities*: Delling, 'ἀρχή', *TWNT* I, 479 (34 ff.), 482 (13 ff.); Foerster, 'ἐξουσία', *TWNT* II, 569, n. 63. *Rulers*: cf. Delling, 'ἀρχή', *TWNT* I, 487 (13 ff.). *Powers*: Grundmann, 'δύναμις', *TWNT* II, 293 f., 297 (12); cf. p. 23 n. 2 above. *Authorities*: Foerster, 'ἐξουσία', *TWNT* II, 562 (5 ff., 17 ff.), 564 (25 ff.).

doctrine as such, the New Testament found the terminology which had been formed and tempered by Jewish thought valuable in the proclamation of its own message.

The psychological argument.—Closely associated with the linguistic evidence are the psychological factors which have played a considerable part in understanding the ideas of spiritual and earthly lordship.[1] The demonic which terrifies men is not a private peculiarity of an individual but a universal, mysterious perversion of the created order which brings men to their knees before the sun and the elements of nature. It is not by accident that the terms 'principalities' and 'authorities' are used in reference to civil government, for while its power is always exercised by individuals in authority, the power exists quite apart from the character of the person as a form of power apparent only in public office.[2]

Schlier concludes that the god of this age is to be found in that which characterizes and distinguishes it as the antipode and perversion of creation, a mysterious and incalculable power which bears the alarming mask of a god and becomes a real 'world ruler', so that the casting out of the lord of this world is actually the world's effective judgment and termination.[3] The restlessness and strife which are normative for the life of the world are founded in the world's unrelenting hold upon itself.[4] Nowhere else than in the

[1] This section reflects especially the contribution of Schlier, 'Mächte', pp. 291 ff.
[2] Cf. Foerster, 'ἐξουσία', TWNT II, 559 f.; Schmidt, p. 11.
[3] Schlier, 'Mächte', pp. 291 f. Cf. Macgregor, pp. 17 f.; Bultmann, I, 256; Sasse, 'κόσμος', TWNT III, C, 4, c, esp. p. 893 (2–14); Wendland, p. 24; Dibelius, p. 135.
[4] Schlier, 'Mächte', pp. 294 f.; Lohmeyer on Col. 2.15; Foerster, 'ἐξουσία', TWNT II, 570 n. 68; cf. Stewart, pp. 295–7; Macgregor, p. 26, Wendland, p. 33.

A recent work on 'liberty, society and government' by George Santayana is entitled *Dominations and Powers* (London, 1951) because of the appropriateness of the relationship between civil government and 'psychic' forces. 'Without the richly charged individual soul, or the souls of a thousand kindred individuals vibrating in unison, circumstances would continue to compose an empty stage, and a landscape without figures. They become political circumstances when human ambition begins to move amongst them, and to enlist them in its service. Society will then become whatever the psychic disposition of its members may tend to make of it' (*op. cit.*, p. 5). In *The Myth of the State* (London, 1946), Ernst Cassirer reviews various theories of myth as they could apply to the State. 'In myth man begins to learn a new and strange art: the art of expressing, and that means of organizing, his most deeply rooted instincts, his hopes and fears' (*op. cit.*, p. 48).

State is man's effort to take his destiny in hand more evident; nowhere else does human incapacity assume such a superhuman aspect of power.[1]

The theological argument.—1. The theological context of the proposed exegesis.—At this point it is vitally important to understand that the new interpretation of Romans 13.1–7 is part of a larger concern which is principally theological.[2] It has served as an illustration and buttress of a broader thesis which has commonly been called '*heilsgeschichtlich*', for it deals with the significance of that historical activity which the New Testament declares to have been for our redemption. The whole matter rests upon extensive studies in the history of the earliest Christian thought, most notably those of Oscar Cullmann, whose *Christ and Time* remains the most effective presentation of the thesis.

That God has from the beginning been at work in human history in a very special manner expresses the full meaning of the New Testament only when it is understood that what occurred in Jesus Christ is not only the turning point of history, but at the same time precisely the central and definitive event in that single thread of revealed divine activity which is actually the purposeful direction and meaning of history. Not only did the earliest believers understand general history from the point of view of redemptive history, but the whole significance of redemptive history, past, present, and future, could be understood only from the viewpoint of the Christ-event.

Research into the basic beliefs of early Christianity has proved the central creed of Christendom and the New Testament to be simply 'Christ is Lord'. The theology of the New Testament has been shown to be first of all Christological, and the first element of this outlook is the lordship of Christ. The reign of Christ was consistently and forcefully proclaimed by the first Christians in terms of his triumph over the 'principalities and powers' which formed so real a part of ancient thought and which have been

---

[1]Peterson, pp. 81 ff.

[2]In *The Kingship of Christ*, Visser 't Hooft has made a clear summary of the theological context within which the proposed interpretation of Rom. 13 has developed; cf. esp. pp. 92–95. Bieder (p. 29 n. 8) like Cullmann (*State*, p. 67) holds that the Christological interpretation of this passage does not rest on the thesis regarding the word *exousiai*. (On the role of theological presuppositions, cf. Bieder, pp. viii f.)

A Positive Contribution

discussed to some extent above. It would be methodologically unsound to consider the lordship of Christ in New Testament thought without taking seriously the form in which it was declared. Likewise it would be unsound to consider Christ's victory over the spiritual powers and yet overlook their obvious linguistic and psychological association with the State.

Thus a satisfactory exegesis of Romans 13.1–7 has become imperative to all who take seriously the form and viewpoint of the New Testament. Furthermore, while the good news of Jesus Christ had manifold relevance to private morality, individual loyalty, religious practice, and personal peace, it was in regard to the State that the lordship of Christ met its supreme test. Any sound exegesis of Paul's views on the State must deal with them theologically.[1] The theological proof of the new interpretation of Romans 13 is based upon a particular view of New Testament theology, and *within* this view it is found to be thoroughly consistent.[2]

2. The State in redemptive history: Christ and the powers.—In view of Paul's understanding of a close relationship between spiritual powers and earthly affairs, as well as the fact that New Testament thought is essentially Christological, our first step to understanding Paul's view of the State must be an appreciation of the relationship between Christ and these powers. In Paul's writings the angelic beings illustrate the remarkable continuity of a Christologically founded *Heilsgeschichte*, for (a) these powers were created in Christ, through him and for him, and in him 'all things' hold together (Col. 1.16 f.), (β) At the midpoint of history these powers were active in the crucifixion of 'the Lord of glory' (I Cor. 2.8), but (γ) in his resurrection they were overthrown (Col. 2.15), yet not destroyed, for (δ) at the present time Christians must actively oppose them (Eph. 6.12 ff.). However (ϵ) they will before the 'end' (I Cor. 15.24 ff.) have their final defeat and (at least partial) destruction at Christ's hand. Since creation the world has not only been the scene of divine activity, but the New Testament insists that at every stage *all things* have been related to Christ (cf. I Cor. 10.4; Heb. 11.26). It is in him alone that their meaning and destiny can be understood, because it is only through him and

---

[1] Cullmann, 'Diskussion', p. 328.
[2] Cf. Barth, *Recht*, pp. 3 ff.; Cullmann, *Confessions*, p. 58; D. Bonhoeffer, *Ethics*, ed. E. Bethge (London, 1955), pp. 292 f.

for him that they exist. The point of real controversy in the *heilsgeschichtlich* interpretation of the New Testament is uncovered when it is explained (ζ) that *now* 'so far as they subject themselves to Christ's kingdom (the spiritual powers) also stand behind the legitimate political powers.'[1] Each of the above points (α–ε) deserves fuller attention when the new thesis regarding the State is tested by the theology of the New Testament.

Paul held that there was an integral relationship between the spiritual powers and earthly rulers which was clearly evident in their simultaneous activity in the death of Jesus (β).[2] It is of importance for us to note that the crucifixion resulted in neither metaphysical dualism nor political anarchy in early Christian thought. These extremes were avoided because the relationship of powers to the State was considered a part of divine order. The death of Jesus was 'a stumbling-block to Jews and folly to Gentiles' because they did not understand that the rulers and authorities were *servants of God, created in Christ and for him*; the Christian view of the State was not merely in the form evident in I Cor. 2.8, but with the theological perspective of Romans 13.1–7.[3]

(α) The Christ-event and the present period.—It is the overwhelming testimony of the New Testament that Christ's death and resurrection resulted in the overthrow of the spiritual powers and his exaltation to a position of authority at the right hand of God (γ).[4] Inasmuch, however, as Christians at present (δ) are considered to be engaged in warfare against those very powers which Christ overthrew, the problem is to define the nature of the 'subjection' of these powers at this time between Christ's resurrection and his final complete conquest.[5] Cullmann believes that he has resolved this problem by describing the present in-between

---

[1] Rom. 13.1–7. Cullmann, *Königs.*, p. 26, *Time*, p. 104. (Cf. Dehn, p. 102; Schweitzer, p. 26; Delling, 'ἀρχή', *TWNT* I, 482 (13 ff.); Grundmann, 'δύναμις', *TWNT* II, 308 (30 ff.), 314 (23 ff.); Bultmann, II, 152 f.)

[2] Cf. pp. 23 f. above on I Cor. 2.6 ff.

[3] Acts 4.25 ff. Cf. Cullmann, *Time*, p. 199 f.

[4] *Ibid.*, p. 151. Note the NT passages based on Ps. 110; cf. I *Clem* 36.5, *Barn.* 12.10, Ignatius, *Trallians* 9.2, Polycarp, *Phil.* 2.1, Justin, *Dial.* 85, Irenaeus, *Heresies* I 10.1. Cf. p. 21 n. 6 above. Cf. Grundmann, 'δέξιος', *TWNT* II, 37 (6), 38 (20 ff.), 39 (12 ff.); Bultmann, II, 152. Reicke (*Spirits*, p. 134) holds that pagans are more easily converted because their patrons, the powers, have already heard the gospel from Christ himself.

[5] Dibelius, p. 199; Macgregor, p. 24.

A Positive Contribution

period of Christ's reign as one of 'tension' ('temporal dualism') between what has already occurred and what is yet to be perfected.[1] Particularly fruitful in this regard is the early Christian distinction between the Kingdom of Christ and the Kingdom of God. The former may be defined as the present period of Christ's rule at the right hand of the Father who 'put all things in subjection under his feet' (I Cor. 15.27 [Ps. 8.7]; cf. Eph. 1.22). The latter Kingdom is yet future, to be established 'when he has destroyed every rule and every authority and power' (I Cor. 15.24). The principalities and authorities were 'subjected' ($\hat{υ}ποτάσσω$), but they have yet to be 'destroyed' ($καταργέω$); only in the Kingdom of God is the tension to be resolved.[2]

In the time between the resurrection and the Parousia of Christ (the spiritual powers) are, so to speak, bound as to a rope, which can be more or less lengthened, so that those among them who show tendencies to emancipation can have the illusion that they are releasing themselves from their bond with Christ, while in reality, by this striving which here and there appears, they only show once more their original demonic character; they cannot however, actually set themselves free. Their power is only an apparent power.[3]

[1] Cullmann, *Time*, p. 153. Contrast I Peter 3.22, Col. 1.16; 2.15; Phil. 2.10 with I Cor. 15.25; Heb. 10.13 ('Diskussion', p. 333). Cf. Dibelius, pp. 201 ff.

[2] Cullmann, *Time*, p. 199; *Königs.*, pp. 11 f.; Künneth, pp. 50 f.; Schweitzer, p. 38; Dibelius, pp. 200 f. It is this representation of the work of Christ as a complete event and yet one not fully realized which suggests to Cullmann not only the idea of 'tension', but the view that the powers are to be defeated *once again* (*Time*, pp. 153, 199; *Königs.*, pp. 16 f., 26; 'Diskussion', p. 333).

[3] Cullmann, *Time*, p. 198. Cf. pp. 196, 202; *Königs.*, pp. 27 f.; Visser 't Hooft, pp. 92–94. Stewart, p. 299 and Macgregor, p. 24, cite P. T. Forsyth, *The Glorious Gospel*, p. 7: 'the wickedness of the world is, after all, a "bull in a net", a chained beast kicking himself to death.' Cf. also Barth, *Recht*, p. 16; Künneth, p. 43. Cullmann uses various expressions for this and at times they do not appear consistent. (*a*) Powers are under the lordship of Christ 'so long as they are subject to him and do not seek to become emancipated from their place in his service' (*Time*, p. 196, cf. p. 202). (*b*) There are times, evidently, when 'the State is in danger of falling out of the divine order' (*ibid.*, p. 204; *Königs.*, p. 27). (*c*) 'So far as they subject themselves to Christ's kingdom, they also stand behind the legitimate political powers' (*Time*, p. 104). (*d*) 'They can for a time free themselves from their bound condition and then show their demonic character' (*ibid.*, p. 202). On the other hand (*ibid.*, p. 198) it is only an 'illusion that they are releasing themselves . . . they cannot, however, actually set themselves free' (cf. *Königs.*, p. 28). This latter view is taken to be Cullmann's more precise opinion in this regard. With (*b*) above, cf. G. Stählin in H. Kleinknecht et al., '$ὀργή$', *TWNT* V, 442 (9–11).

This means that the period of tension is a cosmic condition. Just as sin and death, weeping and longing linger in the earthly sphere of Christ's rule (I Cor. 7.30; Rom. 6.12; 8.23), so the heavenly powers cannot be characterized as absolutely submissive to his lordship. They are at one time both good and bad, good because they have been subjected by Christ's death and resurrection, bad because of their desire to be free from this subjection and to return to their original independence.[1]

This analysis provides the necessary background for resolving the well known contradiction between the State's being at one time the servant of God, maintaining peace and punishing crimes (Rom. 13), and at another time playing the role of the 'beast' with the apparent power to threaten the very existence of the Church (Rev. 13). The contradiction is actually only another aspect of the perplexity and paradox which characterize the era of tension between the affairs of 'this world' and the consummation of what is already to some degree present. Thus while to all appearances the State has broken out of its subjection to Christ, the powers behind it are merely running the length of their leash. If there is any relationship at all between the heavenly powers and earthly authority, then the victory in Christ has put Christians beyond the realm of terror before the rebellious State.[2]

(*b*) *Servants in the Kingdom of Christ.*—Although the powers were defeated and rendered incapable of threatening believers,[3] Cullmann and Barth believe that their survival was intentional. They hold that early Christians believed that the principalities and powers were recommissioned to their ordained vocations, in which they are instrumental to Christ's Kingdom quite apart from their own desires and in spite of their rebellion[4] (ζ).

By their subjection under Christ the invisible powers have rather lost

[1]Cullmann, 'Diskussion', pp. 332 f.
[2]Rom. 8.38. Barth, *Recht*, p. 16; 'Volkskirche', pp. 421 f.; Schweitzer, p. 40; Reicke, *Spirits*, p. 132. It is according to the accepted thought of the time that victory over the State should be accomplished first in the heavenly places.
[3]Barth, *Recht*, pp. 16 f.; Phil. 2.9 f.; Eph. 1.21; I Peter 3.22; Col. 2.15, etc. Barth believes καταργεῖν of I Cor. 15.24 should be translated 'subject' rather than 'destroy' because of the following verse (25). But Cullmann (*Königs.*, p. 17) shows that v. 24 refers rather to v. 26, while v. 25 describes the period of Christ's rule before the end.
[4]Barth, *Recht*, p. 17; Cullmann, *Time*, p. 202; Visser 't Hooft, pp. 93 f.

A Positive Contribution

their evil character, and they also now stand under and within the Lordship of Christ, as long as they are subject to him and do not seek to become emancipated from their place in his service.[1]

This aspect of Paul's view of the powers is particularly significant in regard to the State. The officers of government are designated as servants (διάκονοι) and ministers (λειτουργοί) of God. It is important here to make clear that 'God' in Romans 13 'cannot be severed from the person and work of Christ, he cannot at all be understood as the God of Creation and Providence in general,' which was the understanding of the reformers and subsequent orthodoxy.[2] The early Christians' understanding of the State of any period of time was grounded in their understanding of redemptive history which was consistently Christocentric. Thus the significance of 'God' here is precisely that the State is what it is, not by nature, but by *divine ordinance*. There is no indication that the source of this ordination was accredited according to the Trinitarian formula, least of all that it was intended to designate the Father as distinct from the Son. To the early Church there could be no doubt as to the purpose and end of the State's ordination; it was exactly the same as all else that existed, for 'all things were created through him and for him' (Col. 1.16). The divinely ordered State was a servant, but clearly the servant of the Lord Jesus Christ.

Evidence is not wanting for the view that the angelic powers, and the earthly governments under their authority, were considered servants of Christ in the New Testament and other early Christian writings. The designation of civil officials as servants and ministers of God (Rom. 13.4, 6) is considerably illuminated by the reference in Heb. 1.14 to '*ministering* spirits sent forth to *serve*'. It seems, as Cullmann observes, 'particularly noteworthy that in this passage these "ministering spirits" are expressly identified with the "enemies" cited in Ps. 110, the enemies whom the

---

[1]Cullmann, *Time*, p. 196. Cf. Schweitzer, p. 36: 'The *powers* accordingly, after their disarmament, became members of his body.' As Christ has only one body, then 'they were incorporated into the triumphing Church'. Otherwise Schlier, 'Mächte', p. 296: 'But with their subjection their rebellion immediately began, and it was precisely the judgment over them that drove them to struggle for their lives at any price.' Cf. Schweitzer, pp. 28 f., 44.

[2]This applies also to Schlier and Dehn. Barth, *Recht*, p. 20; Cullmann, *Time*, p. 209; Visser 't Hooft, pp. 92 f.

Christ who sits at the right hand of God "makes the footstool of his feet".[1] Polycarp (*Phil.* 2.1) also identifies the exalted Christ as the one 'to whom are subject all things in heaven and earth, whom all breath serves'.[2] It is actually only because the spiritual powers behind the State are subjected and in the service of Christ, 'members of the Kingdom of Christ', that the State, which they govern, receives its high dignity and is worthy of honour.[3]

(*c*) The rule and servants of Christ in the light of eschatology.—Although defeated, subjected, even servants, the spiritual powers were never really intended to share in the final Kingdom of God (ε). Their function in 'this world' would be altogether out of place in 'the world to come'. Already they have become obsolete as mediators (*to Christians*) of law, religion, and morality because of the work of Christ (Gal. 3.19, 23; 4.9), and this is a strong indication that the eschatological evaluation of the powers of this world by the early Church was always in relation to the 'once-for-all', but not fully realized, victory in the past.[4] However, they remain valid and necessary in the world so long as it remains. The present period of the Kingdom of Christ may be distinguished from the Kingdom of God by the continued validity of the powers as rulers in 'this age', which is under Christ's lordship but which is ignorant of or opposed to his gospel. The Kingdom of God by contrast may be defined by God's presence with his people and their knowledge of him,[5] and that Kingdom's final consummation may be defined in terms of the 'destruction' of the principalities and powers.[6]

[1]Cullmann, *Time*, p. 205, cf. p. 198; *Königs.*, pp. 8, 40; 'Diskussion', pp. 334 f.; Stewart, p. 300; Macgregor, p. 24.
[2]Cullmann, *Königs.*, p. 6; *Time*, p. 114.
[3]*Ibid.*, pp. 200, 202, 204. Cf. *Königs.*, pp. 46 f. Cullmann (*Time*, p. 209) offers additional confirmation of the place of the State in the divine order. The NT does not explain how the State, founded upon recompense (cf. Rom. 12.19 and 13.4), and the Church, founded upon love, come to this understanding, but Cullmann feels certain the 'natural law' is the least likely reason (*Time*, pp. 201-4). Cf. Barth (*Christengem.*, p. 21; ET, p. 31) who feels that at best the State has knowledge *only* of the ideals of 'natural law'. Cf. C. H. Dodd, 'Natural Law in the Bible', *Theology* 49, 1946, p. 133; Wendland, p. 28.
[4]Cullmann, 'Diskussion', p. 328.
[5]Rev. 21, I Cor. 15.28. Cullmann, *Time*, pp. 199 f., cf. p. 208; *Königs.*, pp. 22 f., 26.
[6]Cf. Grundmann, '$δύναμις$', *TWNT* II, 297 (7); Schlier, 'Mächte', p. 290; Cheyne's (1888!) introduction to Ps. 82; see p. 32 n. 3 above. 'The question

A Positive Contribution

What applies to the powers may be applied also to their earthly counterpart, the State. Its purpose is to maintain peace in a world which is given over to strife; it judges between good and evil and executes punishment. The State's work and necessity are definable in terms of the character of 'this world'. Yet the peace which it is to maintain in the world is for a purpose which Christians alone clearly understand. They alone know that civil justice was instituted to aid divine justification, for they alone comprehend the true nature of creation and history. But the work of redemption was not conceived as an infinite programme; preaching the gospel, the work of the Church, and the Kingdom of Christ also were to have an end, and their transformation at the time when God becomes 'all in all' would leave no place for an agency such as the State. The eschatological role of the State, therefore, was conceived in terms of the one great event in the past; when the work of Christ would be fully realized, all powers, and therefore the State, would find their destined termination. The State as a servant of God, like other instruments in the reign of Christ (e.g. a missionary Church), has its *raison d'être* in a context where the work of Christ is not fully realized and the world is characterized by and in the power of the rulers of this age. Thus when the Kingdom of Christ becomes the Kingdom of God, the State will no longer have purpose or substance.[1] It is in light of the worldly state's transitory nature and the citizenship of Christians in an enduring Kingdom that the State rather than the Christian appears as the sojourner.[2]

(*d*) The context of creation.—It is of great significance for New Testament Christology that (*a*) all things were created through Christ and for him. As Cullmann has pointed out, it is this assertion which most clearly reveals the emphatic Christocentric view

---

as to how, according to Paul, the victory of Christ over the spirits in the past is related to the destruction of the spirits in the Messianic Kingdom is not capable of scientific solution' (Dibelius, p. 206).

[1] K. L. Schmidt concludes his study of *polis* by observing that it is eschatology and Christology which ultimately shape the Christian view of the State (*Die Polis in Kirche und Welt*, Basel, 1939, pp. 108–10).

[2] I Cor. 6.1 ff.; Phil. 3.20; Heb. 13.14; 11.13–16; I Peter 1.1, 17; *II Clem.* 5.1, 5; *Diognetus* 6.8; Schlier, 'Staates', pp. 114 f., 118, 314, 329 f., 337 f.; cf. Schweitzer, pp. 34, 48 f.; Schmidt, pp. 11, 13; Jones, p. 419.

of the early Church toward redemptive history.[1] The powers specifically are cited as subordinate to Christ by reason of their creation 'in him', and thus in every way from the foundation of the world they have been part of an order and development in history which is Christ-founded, Christ-centred, and Christ-consummated. This conviction of the New Testament may be clear without being systematic or without answering every question which could be asked. But from what evidence is at hand there appears in Paul's perspective to have been no time, even prior to the life-death-resurrection victory of Christ, when the powers were autonomous or anything other than subjected to him through whom and for whom all things were made.[2]

While the relationship between the State and the powers in this aspect of *Heilsgeschichte* is nowhere specifically set forth, it is confirmed in several ways. The New Testament holds that at no time before Christ was the State unrelated to or independent of the history of redemption. The Old Testament consistently saw the heads of foreign powers as the servants of the divine will, and the New Testament understood this to be nothing other than that plan of redemption revealed and triumphant in Christ.[3] What Paul understood to be Pharaoh's place in God's single purpose (Rom. 9.17) Luke also records as the early Christian understanding of the State in their own time: 'Both Herod and Pontius Pilate, with the Gentiles and the peoples of Israel (did) whatever thy hand and thy plan had predestined to take place' (Acts 4.25 ff.). This work of the State was to no other end than the death of Christ on behalf of believers. The New Testament holds civil authorities in every stage of history, however ignorant they were of the truth, to have been instruments of that one redemptive purpose which is rooted in the creation of all things in Christ, through him and for him.

3. The State in early Christian thought: a summary.—What has been declared concerning the spiritual powers and world

[1]Cullmann, *Time*, pp. 18 f., 131 ff.; Col. 1.16 (comm. by Synge and Masson); cf. John 1.1 ff.; Macgregor, p. 28; Wendland, pp. 26 f.

[2]Col. 1.15 ff. (2.9), I Cor. 8.6; I Peter 1.20; Heb. 1.2, 10 ff.; John 1.3; 17.24. Cullmann, *Time*, p. 104, Part I, ch. 7 (cf. p. 108), Part II, ch. 2 (cf. p. 131), pp. 177 ff., 209 f.; Dehn, p. 102; Foerster, 'ἐξουσία', *TWNT* II, 570 (18 ff., 22); Bultmann, II, 146 ff., I, 302.

[3]Isa. 45.1 ff.; Jer. 25.9 ff. Cf. Fichtner in Kleinknecht et al., 'ὀργή', *TWNT* V, 400 (6–12, 42 f. and n. 140), 405 (6–10); Stählin, *ibid.*, 443 (3–8), but cf. 442 n. 405; Kittel in Grundmann et al., 'ἄγγελος', *TWNT* I, 85 (10 ff.).

A Positive Contribution

rulers from creation until the end of this age has been shown to have a meaningful correspondence when applied to the biblical understanding of the State.[1] At every stage the new interpretation of Romans 13.1–7, according to which the term *exousiai* comprehends both civil and spiritual rulers who are servants of Christ, is thoroughly consistent with the central elements of the early Christian faith.

Among the πάντα ('all things') in heaven and on earth created in Christ were the principalities and authorities unto whom was entrusted the guardianship of the nations. At the appointed time and in accordance with God's will the spiritual powers of the world, whose wisdom was characterized by ignorance of God and whose life was under the domination of death, acting through their agents, the civil authorities, crucified the Lord of glory. But in his resurrection the world's wisdom was shown to be foolishness, its dominating power was broken and discredited, and Jesus Christ was proclaimed as Lord of heaven and earth. From this point in history the purpose of creation and the meaning of history were understood. The institution of civil government could no longer appear arbitrary and the powers which governed men could never, for all their self-will, be thought autonomous. Dualism and fortune alike were exposed as false concepts, for the whole course of history was shown to be effectively directed toward the one end for which all things were created. Subjection of the world to guardians (the establishment of the State, the gift of the Law, etc.) was according to the will of God who created in Christ, through him, and for him.

The Church's calling is to proclaim the gospel in the world; it is the instrument of revelation in redemptive history's *period of tension*. That is, the Church's native environment is one in which men are under guardians, in ignorance, and under the power of sin and death. The Christian mission is carried on precisely in a world where the State is valid and necessary. In short, *the work of redemption, even the proclamation of Christ, cannot be defined in terms*

[1]Cf. G. H. Williams, 'Christology and Church-State Relations in the Fourth Century', *Church History* 20, 1951, No. 3, p. 26. Nicene Christianity held that the state was 'sustained by angelic power under Christ'. In *ibid.*, No. 4, pp. 15 f., Williams shows that the Arian derivation of imperial authority from the supreme God perpetuated royal absolutism. However, cf. No. 3, p. 4; in the ante-Nicene period, the State is always considered an order of creation.

of the Church alone, but only in terms of the Church and the State. In the period of tension the State was ordained (in Christ, through Christ, and for Christ) to provide an environment conducive to the proclamation of the Christian message and its being heard.[1]

This commission, however, is fulfilled in the realm and by the means of the secular exercise of justice, ensuring freedom and peace according to the standards of human understanding and ability.[2] Every government is commissioned to this task and its authority is not limited by its abuse or by the incapacity of the officials,[3] for men 'have never been good, are not, and furthermore never will be'.[4] It is precisely these men, who formed governments and have equipped them with power to ensure their authority, through whom God will realize an indispensable aspect of his historical purpose quite apart from his revelation or their belief.[5] In short, there is no such thing as a 'Christian State', but likewise there is no such thing as a state which is not actually a servant of redemption. The State has no participation in the preaching of the Gospel or sharing in the knowledge of the truth, but its participation in providing peace for the work of the Church is its full part. The State is able to comprehend its duty and to deal justly without any knowledge of its place in redemptive history or any other revealed truth. Likewise the State is of definite service in God's special work in history quite apart from its willingness to conform to its responsibility or even from its rebellion.[6]

But in whatever condition Christians find the State they know (a) that however serviceable it may be, it is always a human enter-

[1] Barth, *Christengem.*, p. 10 (ET, p. 21); cf. *Christliche Gemeinde im Wechsel der Staatsordnungen* (Zollikon-Zürich, 1948), pp. 33 ff.; Künneth, pp. 40, 57, 59.
[2] Barth, *Christengem.*, pp. 19 f. (ET, p. 30).
[3] Schlier, 'Staates', p. 326, cf. pp. 322, 324.
[4] Barth, *Christl. Gem.* p. 36.
[5] Barth, *Christengem.*, p. 14 (ET, p. 25); *Christl. Gem.*, pp. 36, 49; 'Volkskirche', pp. 412 f. Cf. the ἀνθρωπίνῃ κτίσει in I Peter 2.13.
[6] Cullmann, *Time*, pp. 202, 204, 209. Barth, *Christengem.*, p. 21 (ET, pp. 31 f.); cf. Schlier, 'Staates', pp. 323, 325, 330; Künneth, pp. 39, 44 f. This point of view of Barth and Cullmann should be distinguished from the more traditional view which represents the Church and State as 'polarities' (Dehn), or perhaps even as 'two parallel lines' (Schmidt) or grounded in two separate authorities (Schlier). According to the point of view given here, the Church and State both follow the *same heilsgeschichtlich* line and are oriented about the *same* pole of Christ's lordship. Barth, *Recht*, p. 20, 'Volkskirche', p. 413, *Christengem.*, p. 9 (ET, p. 21); Cullmann, *Time*, Part III, ch. 2, esp. p. 188, *Königs.*, ch. 3 and 4. Thus in the Christocentric viewpoint of the NT, the

A Positive Contribution

prise, the instrument of angelic powers, and is never properly evaluated apart from those New Testament passages which see its rebellious potentialities. Christians must always be critical of the State. On the other hand, (*b*) however beastlike its intent toward the Church, the angelic powers behind the State are always finally subjected to Christ, who, as Lord of heaven and earth, sits at the right hand of the Father.[1]

Christian 'subjection' to the State, therefore, is actually proper respect of the State's role in the plan of redemption,[2] supporting the authorities as they exercise judgment upon the good and evil by paying taxes and giving them the honour appropriate to ministers of God.[3] Beyond respect, which is expected of everyone, Christians have the added responsibility of praying for the State, whatever its condition, that it may fulfil its task in God's service, ensuring that 'we may lead a quiet and peaceable life'.[4] It is in prayer for the State that Christians acknowledge its part in the history of redemption and the service of Christ. It is the unique knowledge of the Christian regarding the nature and destiny of the world under Christ which conveys also the will of God that, as a matter of conscience, he should not obstruct or dishonour, but rather respect the State as an effective instrument in the overall plan of God's redemption.

State, as well as the whole doctrine of Creation, must be understood in the light of redemptive history, i.e. the service of Christ who is now Lord. Cf. Barth, *Christl. Gem.*, pp. 47 ff.; *Recht*, pp. 11 f., 31.

[1]Schmidt, p. 15; Cullmann, *Time*, pp. 190 n. 5, 199, 202, cf. p. 193; Barth, *Recht*, p. 12 f., *Christengem.*, p. 9 (ET, p. 21), *Christl. Gem.*, pp. 32 ff.; Künneth, p. 53. Wendland, p. 33. Cf. the dispute between W. Mögling ('Ursprung, Grenze und Aufgabe des Staates', *KrS* 101, 1945, pp. 162–6, 178–80, 194–8, 212–16, and 'Um die Exegese von Römer 13', *ibid.*, p. 278) and C. Eggenberger ('Der Sinn der Argumentation in Röm. 13.2–5', *ibid.*, pp. 243–4). Mögling looks upon Rom. 13 as defining what a state *should be* and thus concludes that when the State ceases to live up to that standard and becomes 'demonic', Christians have no obligation to obey. Eggenberger maintains that Rom. 13 describes the State as it *is*, and thus concludes that a subject's setting the conditions of his subjection voids the idea of subjection and is refusal to accept the State as God's ordinance. This is a classical division. Cf. Bonhoeffer's distinction between government and State and his Christological emphasis (*Ethics*, pp. 297–303).

[2]Künneth, pp. 57–61; cf. Schweitzer, p. 45; Schlier, 'Staates', p. 320.

[3]Cf. I Peter 2.17; Barth, 'Volkskirche', p. 413, *Christengem.*, p. 16 (ET, p. 26).

[4]I Tim. 2.1 ff., cf. *Mart. Polycarp* 10.2 and Polycarp, *Phil.* 12.3; Schmidt, pp. 3, 7; Dehn, pp. 108 f.

II

THE NEGATIVE REACTION

WITH few exceptions (e.g. Schweitzer, Héring, Künneth) the recent interpretation of Romans 13.1–7, which has just been reviewed, has been challenged as a whole and in practically every part.[1] The opponents have for the most part confined their re-

BASIC BIBLIOGRAPHY: G. BORNKAMM, 'Christus und die Welt in der urchristlicher Botschaft', *Zeitschrift für Theologie und Kirche* 47, 1950, 212–26. Emil BRUNNER, 'Zur christologischen Begründung des Staates', *KrS* 99, 1943, 2–5, 18–23, 34–36. Rudolf BULTMANN, 'Heilsgeschichte und Geschichte', *TLZ* 73, 1948, 659–66. Hans von CAMPENHAUSEN, 'Zur Auslegung von Röm. 13: Die dämonistiche Deutung des ἐξουσία-Begriffs', *Festschrift Alfred Bertholet zum 80. Geburtstag*, ed. W. Baumgartner, Tübingen, 1950, pp. 97–113. Oscar CULLMANN, see p. 17. M. DOERNE, 'Gunther Dehn, Unsere Predigt Heute' (a review), *TLZ* 73, 1948, 684 f. Otto ECK, *Urgemeinde und Imperium*, Gütersloh, 1940. Werner ELERT, *Zwischen Gnade und Ungnade*, Abwandlungen des Themas Gesetz und Evangelium, Munich, 1948. Harald FUCHS, *Der geistige Widerstand gegen Rom in der antiken Welt*, Berlin, 1938. Ernst GAUGLER, 'Der Christ und die staatlichen Gewalten nach dem Neuen Testament', *Internationale Kirchliche Zeitschrift* 40, 1950, 133–55. Jean HÉRING, ' "Serviteurs de Dieu." Contribution à l'exégèse pratique de Romains 13.3–4', *Revue d'Histoire et de Philosophie Religieuses* 30, 1950, 31–40. Gerhard KITTEL, *Christus und Imperator: das Urteil der ersten Christenheit über den Staat*, Stuttgart and Berlin, 1939. Johannes KOCH-MEHRIN, 'Die Stellung des Christen zum Staat nach Röm. 13 und Apok. 13', *EvTh* 7, 1947/8, 378–401. W. KÜNNETH, see p. 11. F. J. LEENHARDT, *Le Chrétien doit il servir l'Etat?*, Geneva, 1939. A. OEPKE, 'Irrwege in der neueren Paulusforschung', *TLZ* 77, 1952, 449–58. Otto PERLES, 'Kirche und Welt nach dem Epheser- und Kolosserbrief', *TLZ* 76, 1951, 391–400. K. H. SCHELKLE, 'Staat und Kirche in der patristischen Auslegung von Rm. 13.1–7', *ZNW* 44, 1952/3, 223–3 6. K. L. SCHMIDT, see p. 11. W. SCHWEITZER, see p. 17. G. STÄHLIN in Kleinknecht et al., 'ὀργή', *TWNT* V, 1954. August STROBEL, 'Zum Verständnis von Rm. 13', *ZNW* 47, 1956, 67–93. H.-D. WENDLAND, see p. 17.

[1] Cullmann, 'Diskussion', pp. 321 f., associates the refutation of the thesis between the years 1939–44 with the political situation (specifically the position of Kittel), and observes that the question has received little serious attention recently on its own merit apart from von Campenhausen's essay. Most references are summary judgments based on much older work. The German political situation doubtless had something to do with the early (1934) identification of the *exousiai* in Rom. 13 with the 'world rulers' by K. L. Schmidt (cf. p. 25 n. 2 above).

The Negative Reaction

marks to footnotes in articles on Church and State, the lordship of Christ, particular Greek words, and other related subjects. A few recent commentaries deal briefly with the matter (e.g. Althaus, Gaugler, Michel, Nygren). Many critics only pause to refer to the 'adventurous ἐξουσία-angel-power theories',[1] the 'grotesque misinterpretation',[2] 'the currently fashionable speculation about the spirit-world,'[3] which portrays Paul as a 'political idiot'.[4] With an air of generosity others call it 'very questionable'.[5] The principal extended criticism appears in the philological analysis by Gerhard Kittel, an exegetical-historical treatment by Hans von Campenhausen, a dogmatic-theological discussion by Emil Brunner, and a general reconstruction of the question by Wolfgang Schweitzer.[6] The view of Walter Künneth is particularly noteworthy in that he accepts the new interpretation of Romans 13 as exegetically sound, but feels that this in no way requires him to accept the theological system which until now has been the exclusive guardian of the interpretation.[7] The position of the opponents of the proposed exegesis may be reviewed under the following convenient categories: (*a*) linguistic, (*b*) exegetical, (*c*) historical, (*d*) dogmatic.

CRITICISM OF THE NEW THESIS ON LINGUISTIC GROUNDS

The fact that the term *exousia*, which is used in Romans 13 with obvious reference to civil authorities, is likewise used in most of Paul's catalogues of spiritual powers, has served the recent exegesis as the first cable across the gorge dividing myth and

---

[1] Eck, p. 35 n. 3.
[2] Bultmann, 'Heilsgeschichte', p. 659.
[3] Oepke, p. 453.
[4] Elert, p. 42 and n. 1.
[5] Stählin, p. 441 n. 401. Cf. A. Feuillet, 'Le plan salvifique de Dieu d'après l'épître aux Romains', Part III, *Revue Biblique* 57, 1950, 516 n. 3; Koch-Mehrin, p. 380 n. 9; Otto Michel, p. 283 of his commentary on Rom.; Johannes Munck, *Paul and the Salvation of Mankind*, ET, London, 1959, p. 156 n. 2.
[6] While Schweitzer adopts a positive attitude toward the thesis of ch. I and accepts far more of the *heilsgeschichtlich* evidence than others, his work remains essentially critical of the basic method of interpretation as developed and applied by Cullmann and Barth. Cf. Perles, pp. 399 f.; Doerne, pp. 684 f.; G. Wieser, 'Das christliche Verstandnis des Staates', *KrS* 99, 1943, 149–51.
[7] Künneth, p. 41. Cf. Cullmann, 'Diskussion', pp. 323 f.

history. Upon the establishment of this basic linguistic relationship there followed a complex interweaving of supporting evidence with the result that a bridge of no mean theological significance has been suspended between the spiritual powers and civil authorities. The insecurity of this structure may be shown first of all by examination of the unwarranted linguistic assertion upon which the mass of other evidence was originally dependent.[1]

Exousia itself, singular and plural, is supported by numerous readings which have only a purely political meaning.[2] Of the more than ninety times that the word appears in the New Testament, only eight times does it refer to spiritual powers (Col. 1.16; 2.10; 2.15; Eph. 1.20 f.; 3.10; 6.11 f.; I Cor. 15.24; I Peter 3.22), while three times it clearly indicates civil magistrates (Luke 12.11; Rom. 13.1; Titus 3.1) and numerous references are to authority and power generally (e.g. Mark 13.34; Matt. 8.9; I Cor. 7.37). A close examination finds the first two categories consistently dependent upon their linguistic and substantial context. This leads to the conclusion that the word *exousia* is without a predetermined divine or demonic reference but it derives its meaning from the context.[3]

Just what is the linguistic and substantial context of Romans 13.1–7? Sound New Testament scholarship can affirm the consistency of *exousiai*'s reference to the spiritual powers in Paul's writings, with the exception of Romans 13. This exception, however, should not be alarming as it is throughout manifoldly distinguished from the other passages in which *exousiai* appears. First of all, the linguistic context shows Romans 13, *alone* of all Paul's uses of *exousiai*, characterized by an absence of (1) a catalogue of (at least two) powers, and especially (2) an immediate relationship between *exousia* and its companion term 'principality'. Secondly, from the viewpoint of substantial context, Romans 13 again is distinguished from all other passages using the word *exousiai*[4] as

[1] Kittel, p. 49. Cf. Leenhardt, p. 35 n. 1; p. 36 n. 3; von Campenhausen, p. 98.
[2] Bornkamm, p. 224 n. 2, point 1.
[3] Kittel, p. 50; Leenhardt, p. 35 n. 1; cf. Foerster, 'ἐξουσία', *TWNT* II, 562; Abbott on Col. 2.15. Von Campenhausen (p. 99) insists that the *usual* meaning should be applied when no other is specifically indicated. Also cf. Stählin, p. 441 n. 401; Althaus (commentary, p. 112). Schweitzer does not agree with Kittel (p. 19).
[4] Perhaps Eph. 6.11 f. also should be excepted.

The Negative Reaction

the exception, for it is not in a Christological context. Quite otherwise; there is no reference to Christ whatsoever.[1]

In the light of such exceptional characteristics as these, it would appear that the association of Romans 13 with the other Pauline passages using *exousiai* would constitute considerably more of an exception than would be its association with the popular Greek of the time. The current and ordinary reference of the word, as it appears in Luke 12.11 and Titus 3.1, is to the constituted civil authorities.[2] Further examination of Romans 13 shows each occurrence of the word not only to be isolated from technical terms and modifying clauses which indicate spiritual powers, but *exousiai*, which appears in the plural only in v. 1, is in no extraordinary way to be distinguished from the frequent singular use of the word in the same passage (vv. 1, 2, 3). In short, *exousiai* in v. 1 is the plural use of a word which receives its essential definition from its non-plural use in the passage, and, as is recognized by the protagonists of the new exegesis, the singular is not a technical expression for spiritual powers.

Another term appears in this passage as a synonym for *exousiai*, viz. ἄρχοντες ('rulers') (v. 3). In Paul's time it was an everyday term applying to civil government (Matt. 9.18; Luke 23.13; Acts 16.19). While it *can* have a 'demonic' meaning, as a matter of fact it nowhere in the New Testament has such a meaning apart from a modifying clause (cf. Matt. 9.34; John 12.31; I Cor. 2.6, 8; Eph. 2.2). It is precisely the association of the 'ruler' with 'this world' or 'this age' which identifies it as a spiritual power, and the plurality of the noun is of no decisive significance. When isolated from such a modifying clause or other words which clearly refer to the spiritual powers, there is no evidence that 'ruler' indicates anything other than a state official.[3] Any kingdom, even a demonic one, may have a prince ('principality'), or ruler, or authority, but it does not follow that every prince, etc. belongs to a demonic kingdom.[4]

Examination of the linguistic and substantial context of

[1] Bornkamm, p. 224 n. 2; Wendland, pp. 28 f. Perles (p. 400) agrees with Schweitzer, Dehn, and Schlier in this regard also.
[2] Strobel (Part II) offers an extensive argument on the basis of Luke's usage.
[3] Bornkamm, p. 224 n. 3, points 2, 3. Cf. Althaus.
[4] Kittel, p. 50.

exousia as the proper method of defining a word which otherwise has no clear association with either political or spiritual powers can lead only to the conclusion that *exousia* in Romans 13 must be interpreted in keeping with the common meaning of the term in the Roman world. All lexicons confirm this judgment.[1] The association of *exousiai* with the spirit world came through the influence of the Greek of late Jewish apocalyptic, and there is at present no convincing evidence that Paul relied consistently upon such sources for the understanding of a word which was in common use and of distinctly clear meaning.[2] Although Paul sometimes used the word in reference to the spirit powers and at other times to indicate the governing authorities, it is quite another thing to claim that the word possessed a dual reference, indicating simultaneously the spiritual powers and their earthly counterparts, the politicians. Such a view is unknown to the New Testament.[3]

CRITICISM ON EXEGETICAL GROUNDS

The interpretation of the various New Testament passages which have been proposed to support the new thesis is without exception regarded as inconclusive, if not altogether wrong. I Cor. 2.8, which (in common with Romans 13) employs the key word 'rulers', has been proposed as an example of Paul's comprehending in one event, the death of Jesus, the simultaneous co-ordinated endeavour of both angelic powers and political authorities. This passage is generally considered to offer the most tenable grounds upon which to found the new interpretation, but the proposed exegesis of it is by no means an established or generally accepted one.[4] While 'most modern commentators' generally abandon the interpretation of the 'rulers of this age' as leading political figures,[5]

[1] Kittel, p. 49.
[2] *Ibid.*, pp. 50 f. Cf. von Campenhausen, pp. 99 f.; Gaugler, pp. 145 f.
[3] Althaus; Stählin, p. 441 n. 401; Kittel, p. 51; Gaugler, p. 277; von Campenhausen, p. 104; Strobel, pp. 70 f.
[4] Leenhardt, p. 39 n. 3; Schweitzer, p. 19. Brunner doubts the exegesis (p. 4), but cf. his *Dogmatics*, (ET, London, 1949) I, 233, where he accepts Cullmann's interpretation of the passage but continues to oppose the 'Christological foundation' of the State.
[5] Leenhardt, p. 39 n. 3; Delling, 'ἄρχων', *TWNT* I, 486 ff. J. Schniewind, 'Die Archonten dieses Äons, I Cor. 2.6–8', *Nachgelassene Reden und Aufsätze* (Berlin, 1952), *passim*, with J. Weiss opposes the prevailing view as developed by Everling, Bousset, Lietzmann, and Schlatter. Cf. A. Oepke's rejection also, pp. 452 f.

The Negative Reaction

the attempt to find a direct relationship between the spiritual powers and the political forces, as implied in the concept of folk angels, is drawing too much out of the text.[1] Paul here was not thinking in historical terms but rather in terms of metaphysical drama and spiritual opposition to God's plan of redemption. While it is not contested that Paul perhaps believed that these powers had some influence over the politicians who crucified Jesus, there is no substantiation for a theory that Paul held political authorities to be the terrestrial counterpart of heavenly powers, and their activity merely the projection of a real drama which is essentially heavenly. In the New Testament, heavenly powers and earthly powers are different and distinct, and they must not be confused even if they occasionally are thought to be involved in the same events.[2]

The most strongly opposed element in the exegetical argument involves the interpretation of those passages concerned with Christ's victory over the angelic powers.[3] There is no New Testament evidence whatever to confirm the contention that these hostile powers were in some way harnessed, 're-commissioned', to a positive responsibility in the Kingdom of Christ, and could therefore be called his servants. The passages referring to Christ's victory and lordship affirm essentially that in Christ believers are no longer subject to the spiritual powers of this world. This faith is diametrically opposed to any view that the exalted Christ has recommitted his own to the supervision of 'elemental spirits' or any other kind of spiritual guardians.[4] Rather than appointed servants who have 'lost their evil character', the New Testament is more inclined to look upon these powers as enslaved, for it considers them hostile until they are finally put out of action by Christ's return.[5] Such texts as Rom. 8.38, I Cor. 15.23 ff., and

---

[1] Leenhardt, p. 39 n. 3; Vischer, *op. cit.*, pp. 12, 118; von Campenhausen, p. 100 (after Lohmeyer). Contrast Schweitzer, p. 23.

[2] Leenhardt, p. 40 n. 3. Von Campenhausen (pp. 100 f.) holds that the new view is an improper confusion of historical and mythological concepts, for there is no evidence that *exousiai* or any other word was ever construed in general use to apply to both concepts at once. Cf. Héring, p. 33.

[3] Col. 2.15; Eph. 1.21; I Peter 3.22, etc. Leenhardt, p. 38 n. 3, is unwilling to include Phil. 2.9 with these texts (cf. Cullmann, *Time*, p. 186).

[4] Rom. 8.38; Gal. 4.3; Col. 2.8, 20. Brunner, pp. 4, 18; Leenhardt, p. 37 n. 3.

[5] Cf. von Campenhausen, p. 105 n. 6; Doerne, p. 684 f.; Eph. 6.10 ff.;

Eph 6.11 f. prove Barth, Cullmann, and others to have exceeded the meaning of the New Testament (if not actually opposed it) in their argument for the positive place of the powers in the Kingdom of Christ, for Christians have their primary relationship to him who is the 'head' and not to all sorts of intermediary powers.[1] It is precisely upon this point that von Campenhausen and Brunner believe the whole interpretation of *exousiai* breaks down.[2]

That this interpretation of the powers' conscription to serve the Kingdom of Christ is foreign to the New Testament is apparent in the total lack of evidence to support it.

The only argument offered from an exegetical point of view is in the attempt to relate the 'ministers' of Rom. 13.6 to the 'ministering spirits' of Heb. 1.14. In trying to show that the spirits, which were formerly enemies of God, were subjected by Christ and commissioned with responsibilities in his service, it has been necessary to make the antecedent of 'all' (v. 14) to be 'thy enemies' (v. 13). This identification, however, ignores the whole context of the first chapter of Hebrews, which aims to show that the Son became 'as much superior to angels as the name he has obtained is more excellent than theirs' (v. 4). The author's point is illustrated by several Old Testament passages which he believes were written concerning the Son. In the midst of the lengthy

---

I Cor. 15.24 ff.; Justin, *I Apol.* 45.1. Instead of being enslaved and deprived of their power, the spiritual powers, according to another view, became more ferocious (Schweitzer, pp. 28 f.; cf. p. 33 n. 1 above).

[1]Leenhardt, p. 38 n. 3.

[2]Von Campenhausen, pp. 105 f.; Brunner, p. 4. Schweitzer (pp. 27, 30 ff.) breaks with Barth and Cullmann, maintaining that Paul's concept of the powers' defeat was one of 'unconditional surrender', and that by no means could describe the state of things in the interim period. The lordship of Christ must be understood rather as a 'commission to conflict', and the Christian life is one of spiritual warfare. The Church's proclamation of the word is the means by which Christ, who already reigns in heaven, is to become victorious over the rulers of this world, and victory is eventually to be realized (I Cor. 15.24 ff.). He therefore (p. 56 n. 9) opposes Cullmann's concept of a 'repeated' defeat of the powers at the end, and, by way of simplification, appears to affirm the concept of Christ's absolute lordship and control over a part of the powers (those in heaven) rather than a limited victory over all of them which must be repeated. (Schweitzer however wants to avoid this conclusion, p. 37.) The advantages of this view are that (*a*) the true character of the spiritual powers in this period is recognized and is not obscured by ambivalence; (*b*) the contradiction of a 'once for all' victory followed by a necessary 'repeated' triumph is avoided (cf. p. 31 n. 2); (*c*) when fully realized, Christ's victory will be one worthy of the name.

The Negative Reaction

citation one verse was inserted by way of contrast to make clear the distinction between the Son and the angels of the heavenly court: 'Of the angels he says, "Who makes his angels winds (πνεύματα) and his ministers (λειτουργούς) flames of fire"' (Heb. 1.7). The opening question (v. 5) is repeated in v. 13. The reason God never spoke to angels as he did to the Son is obvious: the *angels* of the heavenly court are merely 'ministering spirits' as was stated earlier in v. 7. The clear identity of the angels with the ministering spirits excludes the possibility of any identity between them and enemies which were defeated. Therefore we must conclude that there is here no reference to the spiritual 'powers of this world' giving positive service to Christ, nor is there in any way an indication anywhere in the New Testament that these powers had been transformed for the better by his work.[1]

That all passages mentioning the principalities and powers were not intended to be systematized seems clear from the ambiguous results of such a system. The letter to the Colossians submits the view that Christ, by reason of the fact that all things were created through him and for him, was Lord over all things from creation. Then at the centre of the New Testament proclamation we find declared that in his death and resurrection a very decisive and significant thing happened: Christ became victorious and Lord over the principalities and powers. Finally it is obvious that these enemies are yet active and he must defeat them ('again') in the future. This assembly of evidence is even more awkward from the viewpoint of the powers: Since creation they have never been fully free to realize anything other than the will of *Christ*. While in this subdued state they were *decisively defeated*, with the result, however, that they are *still free* to will disobedience and to persecute the elect in a way obviously just the same as before the victory. From this systematization of New Testament evidence it appears either that Paul did not intend his Christological expressions concerning the powers to be systematized, or else what occurred in the Christ-event did not amount to very much. It is clear that the new interpretation of Romans 13 has derived its strength from a form of exegesis which has marshalled its evidence (that which has to do with the angelic powers, at any rate) into an essentially artificial system. This is particularly evident in regard to the passages in Colossians.[2]

[1] Cf. von Campenhausen, p. 106. Cf. Doerne, p. 684.
[2] Schweitzer, pp. 30 ff.; Doerne, p. 684; Strobel, pp. 69–71.

As a positive contribution in refutation of the new thesis, Kittel presents I Peter 2.13–17 as the oldest known reference to Rom. 13. Quite apart from the problem of the original and ultimate divine source for the institution of order among men, this statement clearly avoids any implication of demonic powers; the point of view of proper Christian subjection to established authority, as earlier set forth by Paul, is maintained here with all of its original practical concern and direct simplicity. *The Martyrdom of Polycarp* (10.2) further supports the obvious, non-ambiguous interpretation of Paul's words: 'For we have been taught to render honour . . . to princes and authorities appointed by God.' Early witnesses of this sort, which make clear the Christian attitude toward the State, must be placed alongside the words of Irenaeus: '*He spoke these words, not in regard to angelical powers, nor of invisible rulers—as some venture to expound the passage—but of actual human authorities*' (*Heresies* v 24.1). Thus it becomes clear that there is little ground for the contention that the heresy under attack necessarily reflects the 'earliest' form of the Christian understanding of the State. On the contrary, it appears more obvious that the view opposed by Irenaeus, i.e. that the State is under the authority of spiritual powers, is a characteristic element of gnostic thought.

Von Campenhausen's positive contribution to the exegesis of Romans 13.1–7 is more detailed. Rather than being rooted in angelology, the whole context of this passage speaks for an eschatological orientation.[1] A true parallel to the content of Romans 13 may be found in I Thess. 5. Both passages are concerned with (*a*) anticipation of the great day of the Lord, doing good, not recompensing vengeance upon one's enemies, but especially (*b*) the necessity of subjection under the present order which is established by God and under his rule. The dissimilarity between the church officials (I Thess.) and civil officials (Rom.) shows that Paul's point is made as part of a general warning against a rebellious and 'unordered' life, which was evidently a temptation to Christians anticipating the Parousia.

Relatively little effort is devoted to disproving the proposed theory on the basis of Romans 13.1–7 itself, chiefly because the

---

[1] Von Campenhausen, pp. 107 ff.; however cf. Cullmann, 'Diskussion', pp. 323 f.; Wendland, p. 28.

The Negative Reaction

new exegesis is founded for the most part on external evidence. Certain facts should be summarized, however. First, it appears to be a most unlikely text upon which to base a strongly Christological interpretation, inasmuch as there is no reference at all to Christ,[1] and every implication is that what is said concerning the authorities is valid quite independently of the work of God in Christ. This is certainly clear from the clause: '. . . and those (authorities) that exist have been instituted by *God*.'[2] Secondly, as stated above, *exousiais* in v. 1 is clearly the plural use of a word which receives its definition in this passage from its singular form and from a context which has to do with civil officials. Thirdly, the word 'servant' and 'minister' cannot be forced to imply any kind of submission or obedience as a result of the victory of Christ, for the idea of a pagan king's unwitting serviceability to the will of God was held in the Old Testament. Kings and nations serve God because he is the Creator and Ruler of history.[3] In short, nothing new relating to Romans 13.1-7 itself has been established. On the contrary, exponents of the new interpretation have had to be satisfied with an attempt to prove that their view is not excluded by the passage. Consequently the traditional exposition must remain as the only scientifically sound treatment of the passage.

In every instance the passages cited by the proponents of the new thesis have required something more than what is usually held to be their actual meaning. There appears on the one hand no single place in the New Testament where the doctrine proposed is clearly evident, and on the other hand every passage involved in the exegetical discussion is perfectly intelligible apart from the rather ambiguous interpretation which the *Heilsgeschichte* school places upon it.[4]

CRITICISM ON HISTORICAL GROUNDS

The historical novelty of this new thesis is emphasized particu-

---

[1] Bornkamm, p. 224 n. 2; Brunner, p. 13.
[2] V. 1; Θεός appears six times in the seven verses.
[3] Gaugler, pp. 145-7; Michel follows Strack-B (Rom. 13.1-7) citing Dan. 2.21, 37 f.; 4.14 (17); Wisd. 6.1-11; En. 46.5; cf. Jer. 21.7; 29.7; cf. also pp. 19 n. 4 and 36 n. 3.
[4] Von Campenhausen, pp. 100, 111 f.; Leenhardt, p. 37 n. 3; Brunner, p. 4; Althaus.

larly by von Campenhausen.[1] Efforts to show that a close association of demonic powers and political figures is not foreign to the history of Christian interpretation are not well attested and are contrary to the 'classical understanding' of Paul's political thought.[2] Cullmann's appeal to a gnostic exegesis of Romans 13 handed down by Irenaeus[3] (who was opposing it) as a 'typical combination' of the demonic and political meaning of *exousiai* is unjustified, for the gnostic interpretation of Romans 13 made reference not to political but to demonic powers with the manifest purpose of avoiding political obedience. Thus the typical combination does not appear at all and there are no grounds for believing this view in Irenaeus to be the remnant of an older Christian tradition which associated the political and demonic meanings.[4]

The ancient Church varies as to its interpretation of I Cor. 2.8; more adopt the simple political meaning than the demonic, but nowhere does the 'modern' combination of both concepts appear. Likewise the concept of folk angels is of no benefit here, for the ambiguous character of their subjection and rebellion, attributed to them by Barth and Cullmann, is foreign to the earliest Christianity, for whom the distinction between the angels who served God and the fallen demons was not confused.[5]

The effort to show (chiefly by theological analysis) the appropriateness of Pilate's place in the second article of the creed to be a confirmation of the Christological character of the State is sharply denounced. Pilate appears in the second article merely because as a matter of historical fact he was involved in the death of Jesus. It is precisely when the 'mythological' interpretation of the State's activity is introduced that the mention of Pilate becomes thoroughly repugnant and historically isolated.[6]

---

[1]Von Campenhausen, pp. 100 ff.; K. L. Schmidt, who supports the new thesis, admits that he is not concerned so much by modern objections as by the lack of mention by ancient commentators of the identification of angels and *exousiai* as related to civil rulers (p. 15).

[2]Leenhardt, p. 37 n. 3.

[3]*Heresies* v 24.1; Schelkle, pp. 225 f.

[4]Cf. Schweitzer, p. 59 n. 27; von Campenhausen, p. 101 n. 2; Cullmann, 'Diskussion', p. 325. Cf. Origen's spiritual interpretation which 'strangely' has not been cited by the proponents of the new thesis (von Campenhausen, p. 103; Schelkle, pp. 224 f., 227).

[5]Von Campenhausen, pp. 103–5.

[6]Cf. ibid., pp. 100 ff.

The Negative Reaction

The new interpretation has forsaken the clear and obvious historical relationships of Paul's exhortation to be subject to the State in favour of attributing the authority of the government officials to angelic powers more or less subjected by Christ. The new element in Romans 13 is the clarity and vigour of Paul's presentation, for the obvious meaning of the passage is rooted in old Jewish tradition which understood the power of foreign rulers to be from God and so counselled subjection. Beyond this the protagonists of the angel theory have overlooked the practical moral significance which civil justice held in rabbinical literature. There is actually nothing surprising in the content of our passage: obedience, divine institution, and moral function. The strikingly Christian element is the earnestness with which Paul pressed the duty of recognizing the will of God in civil ordinance.[1]

In short, opponents of the new interpretation find it to be an irresponsible employment of ancient concepts of angels to promote historically impossible conclusions.[2]

CRITICISM ON DOGMATIC GROUNDS

While dogmatic formulations and conclusions are not our primary concern, they deserve mention in the arguments of the negative view toward the new interpretation of Romans 13 because they embody the traditional perspective of men who have for centuries sought to interpret this passage.

The basic offence to traditional theology has been the seeming disregard shown by the new thesis for the Trinitarian structure of its system.[3] Not only reformed tradition but also Paul founded his doctrine of the State upon the first, not the second, person. Jesus Christ is not even mentioned in Romans 13.1-7. Nowhere does the Son appear clearly as the founder of the State, nor is the emperor declared to be his servant. There is no reference to Roman Law as his gift nor to the sword as symbolizing the 'wrath of *Christ*'.

Is it the case in the Bible that generally where it reads 'God', 'Jesus Christ' could appear just as well, and is then a teaching which in a particular place consciously and persistently says 'God' and not 'Jesus

[1] *Ibid.*, pp. 106 f.
[2] *Ibid.*, p. 104.
[3] Cf. Cullmann, *Time*, p. 26 n. 9. Perles, p. 400; Doerne, pp. 684 f.

Christ' to be branded as 'natural theology' or non-Christologically founded theology?[1]

Romans 13 and John 19 both reflect the idea that the works of God are essentially two, *natural* and *redemptive*.[2] All creation belongs to one realm while those who in faith are Christ's belong to the other. The State does not belong to the redemptive sphere with the Church, but it does belong to the natural order established by God, and for this reason the Christian honours it.[3] A Christological teaching of creation may be found in Colossians and Ephesians, and the State may be included in that picture, but it remains nevertheless a teaching concerning *creation*.[4] Thus a thoroughly Christological theology may be concerned, under certain circumstances, with God alone and not with Jesus Christ, for there are spheres, such as the State, which belong not to the Son, but only to his Father.[5]

---

[1] Brunner, p. 18; cf. Doerne, pp. 684 f.; Schweitzer, p. 45 n. 37; cf. p. 38 n. 6.

[2] Brunner, p. 20; Schweitzer, p. 24.

[3] It should be noted here that since the early and rather academic theological opposition to the new interpretation (also see p. 40 n. 1 above), theologians, especially in Germany, have come to the question of the Christian and the State in the light of actual problems. The result has generally been one of gratitude to Barth and Cullmann (e.g. Perles, pp. 397 f.) and increasing favour toward the new exegesis although seldom its complete adoption. This favourable attitude falls roughly into two categories. (*a*) The doctrine of the two realms must be re-evaluated in the light of the New Testament emphasis upon the universal cosmic lordship of Christ. This has resulted in casting the two realms in the form of Cullmann's two concentric circles and recognizing Christ as Lord of all, including the State. Consequently these recent writers oppose the position of Brunner and Héring as set forth in the text above as not only unbiblical but a perversion of the doctrine of the two realms (Künneth, pp. 72 ff.; Wendland, p. 34; Perles, pp. 396, 398; cf. Anders Nygren, 'Luthers Lehre von den zwei Reichen', *TLZ* 74, 1949, 6–8. (*b*) There is a close relationship between the spiritual powers and the political order, and 'demonic' political circumstances are comprehended in terms of 'this world'. Thus a new understanding of the tension and conflict of the present time as well as the purpose and end of both Church and State is sought with a new Christological and eschatological awareness. There nevertheless remain several differences between these recent writers and those who proposed and developed the new interpretation of Romans 13 and they are noted in the course of this chapter. Cf. W. A. Whitehouse, 'The State and Divine Law', *Reformation Old and New*, A Tribute to Karl Barth (London, 1947), pp. 199–217; Brunner, pp. 4, 21; Héring, pp. 34 f.

[4] Schweitzer, p. 33.

[5] Brunner, p. 19 f.; cf. Schweitzer (p. 38): 'The State is able to serve the Lord of this Cosmos instead of serving the Lord Jesus.'

The Negative Reaction

In Romans 13, Paul in no way distinguishes his teaching as peculiarly Christian, and the history of religions proves him to stand firmly upon the tradition of prophetic, apocalyptic, and wisdom literature. This tradition of God's appointment and use of rulers for his own purposes is not only a more direct and simple basis for understanding Paul's words, but it is explicitly set forth in the Bible, and the hypothetical interpretation is not. This traditional basis is all the more likely because Paul nowhere hints that the State before Christ was unestablished or godless.[1]

The weakness of the theological basis of the proposed exegesis is evident not only in the direct contradiction of the New Testament mentioned above—i.e. Christ is everywhere declared to have liberated us from the domination of the powers and elemental spirits and nowhere said to have re-subjected us to them—but in a number of logical and practical contradictions as well. For example, association of the State with the demonic powers hardly makes a sound case for honouring civil officials; it is far more likely to foster civil disobedience and fanaticism, for there is no evidence of an early Christian doctrine that these powers are anything but evil and hostile to the Church as long as they exist. Since the New Testament says explicitly that there are some powers yet to be subjected by Christ (I Cor. 15.25, 28; Heb. 2.8b), what evidence is there that the folk angels are not among those yet at large? The Jews appear to have held that Satan himself was the Roman folk angel;[2] is there any New Testament doctrine which declares Satan to have been converted, or that Christians should be subject to him? If we are to suppose that the State became honourable because it crucified Jesus, must we not likewise honour Judas? Nowhere in the biblical tradition do the instruments of God's wrath or judgment become honourable because of their service.[3] Nor can Christian theology afford wholly to ignore actual experience. As a matter of fact the work of Christ, especially his victory over the powers, had no direct effect upon the State; Roman government was the same the day after the resurrection as the day before. The Roman State's preservation of order was without any conscious relationship whatever to the

---
[1] Gaugler, pp. 145-7.
[2] Gaugler, p. 146; Strack-B, I, 141, II, 707.
[3] Brunner, p. 3.

Church and its mission. There is no experience to certify the hypothetical doctrine that the nature of the State was radically altered by the Christ-event or that it had become an instrument in the work of redemption.[1] Rather the Christian view of the State must be founded upon the fact that the Christian respects and honours what he clearly recognizes to be a work of God quite distinct from that which God has wrought in Christ and through the Church.[2]

[1] Schweitzer, p. 44; Héring, pp. 32–34; Brunner, p. 4.
[2] Brunner, pp. 4, 20 f.; Héring, pp. 33–35.

III

AN EVALUATION AND PROSPECT

THE preceding chapters have made clear the manifold disagreement between the proponents of the recent interpretation of Romans 13.1-7 and their critics. The differences are broad and deep; the gulf between them is real and fundamental. Though it may be spanned at a few places, a complete resolution of the conflicting interpretations cannot be expected on the basis of the evidence in hand. The purpose of this chapter is to make clear what elements in the controversy over Romans 13 are agreed upon, and, after evaluation of the remaining points of difference, to outline the problems for consideration in the next section of this work.

THE COMMON GROUND OF AGREEMENT

It will be recalled that the new exegesis is seriously concerned with the spirit-world in Paul's thought. The first striking point of agreement is in this realm. Quite apart from the effort to interpret Paul's words concerning the State in terms of late Jewish thought, there has been no disagreement as to the structure of the universe or the nature of spiritual beings as held by the Jews of the Hellenistic period. In fact there is much agreement regarding the place contemporary cosmology had in Paul's thought. All agree that Paul must have known and to a great extent depended upon the knowledge of the world which he inherited as a Hebrew of the Hebrews and as a Roman citizen of the first century.[1]

The only significant disagreement regarding the vocabulary of the spirit world is the central one: the meaning of *exousiai* in Romans 13. As a result of this disagreement the usage of all the

---

BASIC BIBLIOGRAPHY: DEISSMANN and DIBELIUS, see p. 11. SCHELKLE, see p. 40. SCHWEITZER, see p. 17.

[1] Cf. Dibelius, *Paul*, pp. 15 ff., 27 f., 110; Deissmann, *Paul*, pp. 41 ff., 70, 77 f.

The Powers That Be

other words has been examined with regard to their general consistency and particular context without discovering important differences.[1]

The importance of this agreement (or at least lack of strife) on the nature of the Jewish concept of the spirit world suggests that while not every relevant text or aspect of Jewish thought concerning the spirit world and the State has been set forth in the course of our controversy, on the other hand not a great deal may be expected for the solution of the question by adding more references to the heap already known. The catalogue seems sufficiently full at this stage as far as this particular problem is concerned, and, however well defined may be our knowledge of Jewish speculation, it has not yet made any significant step toward the solution of the main exegetical problem which confronts us, namely: what was Paul *communicating* in Romans 13, especially with regard to the *exousiai*? Consequently we feel that the area for research lies beyond the sphere of Jewish reflection concerning the spirit world and the State, upon which so much discussion has centred in the effort to establish whether or not Paul held the view which has been proposed. Inasmuch as the passage in hand is from a letter, the central question is not whether Paul held such a view —he held many views not evident in Romans 13—but whether he was communicating it.

Perhaps less noted but none the less significant is the agreement, first, that there is, as such, no explicit New Testament doctrine of folk angels. Secondly, the proponents fully concede that the State, as minister (of Christ), has no special revelation concerning its own meaning, but it considers itself to be a human enterprise, or, at most, a servant of other gods. Thirdly, Romans 13.1–7 is eschatologically oriented.

UNRESOLVED DIFFERENCES

The categories used in the second chapter conveniently present the field of controversy which remains unresolved. Here we ask what the merit of each argument is and what is required before a solution can be reached.

---

[1]The disagreement over such passages as I Cor. 2.8 and 6.1 ff. is not particularly linguistic but more broadly 'exegetical'. See the exegetical section below.

An Evaluation and Prospect

1. The *linguistic* aspect of the problem illustrates the general frustration of the argument. The strong point of the affirmative, that the plural of *exousia* is *consistently* used by Paul to indicate the spiritual powers, is countered by the negative observation that everywhere *except in Romans 13* the context supports the spiritual interpretation of the word. In Romans 13, however, the word appears to be defined by its singular meaning in a context which has to do only with civil government. Yet the very fact that the names of the spiritual powers were chosen from the vocabulary which deals with government forbids the artificial rule of context from excluding an idea which must necessarily be considered because of the key-word's very presence. This tack has led von Campenhausen to note that the only real ground remaining for the affirmative's linguistic argument is to maintain that the concept of civil government was, by the nature of ancient thought, inseparable from that of spiritual powers. Schmidt and Reicke affirmed that this was precisely the relationship in the Graeco-Roman period, while von Campenhausen denied it.[1]

The linguistic argument, consequently, has evolved into something quite different from the word-counting science practiced by Dehn and Kittel earlier in the controversy; it has become subordinate to the larger consideration: how generally understood and widely accepted was the concept of spiritual powers behind civil government? Was such a concept so basic to the thinking of the late Hellenistic period that concern with the State, as well as the symbols applied to it, necessarily involved transcendent powers?

So long as we are concerned with the exegesis of a *communication to Rome* we cannot limit ourselves to the thought world of Judaism any more than we can be confined to the range of oriental languages. To ask only what *exousiai* meant for Paul or for Judaism is to overlook the very character of communication. *Exousiai in Romans 13 meant to Paul precisely what Paul thought it would mean to the church at Rome.*

Therefore, we must inquire into Paul's understanding of the Graeco-Roman world. If his Greek word usage had ever been limited to his Jewish background and experience, which is doubtful, it must have undergone a radical revision before the writing

[1] See above pp. 22 n. 1, 21 n. 2, 45 nn. 1 and 2.

of this epistle. His travels as well as his residence in the cosmopolitan Hellenistic cities of Ephesus and Corinth had brought him into contact with the Gentile world in all its variety, and his ministry depended upon his effective communication with those to whom he was sent (I Cor. 9.22); the author of Romans was no amateur. In the course of the next chapter we must inquire further into the meaning of communication for the exegesis of Romans 13.

2. Perhaps the most weighty specific *historical* evidence in opposition to the proposed thesis is Irenaeus' contention (*Heresies* v 24.1) that the angelic powers were not intended by Paul in Romans 13. In the course of the growth of the gnostic cult and its threat to the Church the necessity of defining the Christian faith became increasingly acute with regard to those once general concepts which had acquired a special significance for gnosticism. Irenaeus' statement certainly does not prove that the concept he attacks had ever in any form been used by the Christian Church. It only makes clear that he felt that some Christians were in danger of subscribing to an erroneous teaching which could have serious consequences for them as well as the Church. But on the other hand, his statement that Christians do not share in what obviously had come to be identified with a non-Christian religion does not preclude Paul's having employed a very similar conception at an earlier time when the cosmological basis for it was little more than a 'scientific' fact which would naturally be employed by anyone attempting to understand the world in which he lived. In short, Irenaeus' statement appears to have been accorded far greater weight with regard to determining Paul's thought than it merits. It makes clear only what is obvious on other grounds: the Christian Church does not appear to have considered Paul's statement in Romans 13 to have been a declaration with regard to the nature of the world or its relationship to invisible powers. With no tradition to this effect, Irenaeus can oppose the gnostics' use of the passage to their own ends. This, of course, does not mean that Paul necessarily appealed for Christians to subject themselves to the pagan state without having any more concern for the spirit world than do his twentieth century readers.[1]

There is actually more awareness of the spirit world and its

[1] On the problem of *Traditionsgeschichte* in Irenaeus' judgment, cf. Schelkle, p. 226.

An Evaluation and Prospect

relation to the State on the part of the early Church than the opposition has been willing to admit.[1] These references, however, are open to the same general observation as has been made concerning the New Testament: there is no explicit doctrine of folk angels or other specific evidence of the new theory. At this point we encounter stalemate: to those convinced of the proposed theory the patristic references seem to be a clear indication that such a concept was 'understood' in the early Church. The critics find 'no clear evidence', 'no explicit doctrine'.

This state of affairs is not without significance. Inasmuch as no mass of evidence of the sort submitted thus far will convince the unpersuaded, the future task amounts to something more than indexing patristic and New Testament allusions to the spirit world. If the proposed exegesis is to be proved valid, then there must be demonstrated for the documents of the early Church precisely what is required concerning the words used in the New Testament, namely that there was no need to be more specific than the early writers were. Would an explicit statement concerning the relationship between the spirit world and civil government have been beside the point, not only as a digression from the central task of the writers, but as an unnecessary explanation of what could be assumed? Again it is apparent that the perspective from which future inquiry must be made is in realizing the problem of *communication*. From the viewpoint of the historian this means more than scanning the documents of the early Church, the indexes of subjects, words, and scriptural citations. It involves an understanding of the ancient mind. In writing to Rome Paul could not make the same presuppositions he made in writing to his own churches. But he had to make assumptions in order to write at all. From his knowledge of Jew and Greek in the Hellenistic world, Paul could make assumptions which were not conjectures or inferences. They were what a wide experience had taught him to be an acceptable basis for communication of the gospel in his time.

3. *Exegesis* has not been able to produce an explicit doctrine to accompany the new interpretation of Romans 13. The closest the affirmative has been able to come is in its interpretation of I Cor.

---

[1] Cf. pp. 21 n. 6 and 23 n. 2.

2.8.[1] Almost unanimous acceptance by the critics that the 'rulers' are spiritual powers is especially significant in light of the fact that these critics are uncertain as to the relationship of the transcendent drama to the historical fact. Consequently the critics of the new thesis must now assume some 'burden of disproof', for the affirmative side of the controversy has maintained Paul's acceptance of a relationship between the spirit world and the governing authorities which is well-founded in the religion of Judaism. To deny the validity of this analysis without setting forth a plausible alternative appears arbitrary. The clearest effort by the negative[2] in this direction is the radical denial of any relationship whatever between the spirit world and civil government. That is to say, this passage has the characteristics of a pure myth, and Paul was under no obligation to suppose that there was a causal relationship between powers and the State. The assertion that this is pure myth cannot be seriously considered, however, for the fact that the powers *crucified* the Lord of glory associates their activity with that of particular historical persons.

We are yet far from the solution which is needed, however, for our concern is Romans 13, where any association whatever between the State and spiritual powers is strongly denied by the critics. Furthermore, Romans 13 has to do, not with the death of Christ, but, according to the affirmative, with his lordship over all things. While there may have been a place for the spirit world in the political manoeuvring which led to the crucifixion, there is little help here in understanding that complex problem of the place of the spiritual powers after their defeat, in an age when Christ rules and yet Christians are engaged in spiritual warfare and are not free from civil persecution. I Cor. 2.8, however, has shown well enough that the present discussion is not wholly improbable or irrelevant.

The great problem which remains to be ironed out is complex: (1) It is of particular significance to observe that the close relationship between the State and the spiritual powers which has until now been considered almost exclusively in terms of late Jewish

[1] I Cor. 6.1 ff., which has much to be said for it, has not received any significant discussion. While its presuppositions are clearly affirmative, a catalytic agent is required before it will prove persuasive. The one unfortunate entry in the exegetical controversy was Heb. 1.14.

[2] Cf. pp. 44 and n. 2, 45 and n. 2.

An Evaluation and Prospect

thought appears in a letter to a conspicuously Gentile church. I Cor. 2.8 forces upon us the question: Was the concept of a close relationship between spiritual powers and civil government so limited a concept as both sides of the controversy seem to think it was? Can we assume that a peculiarly Jewish doctrine of folk angels was part of the elementary indoctrination of converted Gentiles and that Paul could therefore rely upon their understanding his Jewish allusions? This problem raises another. (2) The question which hitherto has been foremost in the discussion—Did Paul conceive of the State in terms of the powers and Christ's lordship over them?—is inescapable in testing the theory which has been set forth, but it is essentially a question concerning Paul, not Romans 13. We would ask rather, *did this doctrine underlie Paul's communication to Rome in chapter 13?*

4. The *theological* argument cannot be resumed in the same terms used in chapter II, for we cannot afford the very real danger of superimposing upon exegesis categories foreign to the passage in hand, if not actually to the New Testament as a whole. There is an artificiality in references to the New Testament doctrine of the 'two realms' or of the 'Trinity'. Schweitzer's statement (p. 38) 'that the State is able to serve the Lord of this Cosmos instead of serving the Lord Jesus' illustrates the danger of applying dogmatic categories to an exegetical problem. The validity of a theological conclusion does not necessarily validate the exegesis offered in its support, but sound exegesis should lead to an understanding of Paul's thought and his intention in writing Romans 13.1–7. The theologians have asked some penetrating questions, nevertheless, and these will be given their proper place, but the theological significance of this study must remain primarily exegetical.

The theology of this passage arises from the practical significance of Paul's words to Christians in first-century Rome. How did men who confessed Christ as Lord look upon the mighty rule of Rome? Did the Christ-event in any way affect the State, their relationship to, or understanding of it? Could the Roman State be conceived as a 'servant of Christ' and yet be ignorant of him, or refuse to believe in him? Was the dignity of the State in the eyes of Christians basically related to Christ's lordship? In particular: *was the State in any way related to the spiritual powers in the view of the readers of Romans*? If so, then there is a direct significance in the New Testament's central confession of Christ's lordship for our understanding of the State, and no prefabricated view of two realms can discredit it.

But the significance of Christ's victory and lordship over the powers is far from settled. Were they annihilated or only defeated? Is the decisive battle behind, ahead, or in progress? Are the powers bound fast, on a leash, or still at large? Has their 'attitude' been altered? Are they obedient servants, driven slaves, pirates, or an aroused and more hostile foe? Are Christians freed from the powers or yet subject to them under a new commission?

While these latter questions arise in connexion with our principal problem, they must remain subordinate to it. If a clear contribution can be made toward the exegesis of Romans 13.1–7 by resolving the stalemate on the question of the State's relationship to the spiritual powers, the future discussion of these other problems will be decisively affected.

This summary of contemporary controversy over Romans 13 and survey of the problems yet in the way of a satisfactory solution points consistently to the necessity of taking seriously the problem of communication. It is this approach to the whole question which seems the one most likely to break the stalemate which now grips the linguistic, exegetical, and historical efforts toward an answer. The next section of our essay is concerned with understanding the term *exousiai* in the broader sense of Paul's communication with the Roman church.

Part Two

AN EXEGETICAL CONTRIBUTION TO THE INTERPRETATION OF ROMANS 13.1-7

IV

TO THE ROMANS

COMMUNICATION AND EXEGESIS

THE last chapter has made clear the stalemate which has been reached in the debate regarding Romans 13.1-7. In addition, we have seen that there is another level, practically unconsidered thus far, upon which the question might be reopened and some advance toward a satisfactory solution made. Considered linguistically, exegetically, and historically, the task before us appears repeatedly to be essentially the same: *Romans 13.1-7 must be understood as part of a communication.*

BASIC BIBLIOGRAPHY: F. ANDRES, 'Daimon', *Pauly-W*, Sup. Bd. III, 1918. S. ANGUS, *The Religious Quests of the Graeco-Roman World*, London, 1929. Ernest BARKER, 'Greek Political Thought and Theory in the Fourth Century', *CAH* VI, 505-35. Emile BRÉHIER, *Les idées philosophiques et religieuses de Philon d'Alexandrie,* Paris, 1908. M. P. CHARLESWORTH, 'Some Observations on Ruler-Cult, especially in Rome', *HTR* 28, 1935, 5-44. C. N. COCHRANE, *Christianity and Classical Culture*, Oxford, 1940. Franz CUMONT, *Astrology and Religion among the Greeks and Romans*, New York and London, 1912; *The Oriental Religions in Roman Paganism*, ET, Chicago, 1911. Adolf DEISSMANN, *Light from the Ancient East*, ET, rev. ed., London, 1927; *Paul*, A Study in Social and Religious History, ET,[2] London, 1926. M. DIBELIUS, *Paul*, ed. and completed by W. G. Kümmel, ET, London, 1953. C. H. DODD, *The Bible and the Greeks*, London, 1935. W. S. FERGUSON, 'The Leading Ideas of the New Period', *CAH* VII, 1-40. A. M. J. FESTUGIÈRE, *La révélation d' Hermès Trismégiste:* I, *L'astrologie et les sciences occultes,*[2] Paris, 1950. Floyd V. FILSON, *The New Testament against its Environment* (SBT 3), London, 1950. Henri FRANKFORT, *Kingship and the Gods*, Chicago and London, 1948. T. R. GLOVER, 'The Daemon Environment of the Primitive Christian', *Hibbert Journal* 11, 1912/13, 153-67. Erwin R. GOODENOUGH, *By Light, Light:* the Mystic Gospel of Hellenistic Judaism, London, 1935; *Jewish Symbols of the Graeco-Roman Period* (Bollingen Series 37), I-III, New York, 1953; 'The Political Philosophy of Hellenistic Kingship', *Yale Classical Studies* 1, 1928, 53-102; *The Politics of*

The Powers That Be

What does it mean to interpret Romans as a communication? The most obvious answer is: to grasp by all our skills what Paul was imparting to the Roman church. The important thing to observe in this regard is that there is no noteworthy disagreement among interpreters of Romans 13 as to what the point of the passage is. Paul brought up the subject of the *exousiai* not so much to complete a theological thesis as to appeal to the Romans with regard to the practice of the Christian life at the dawn of a new era, in the place where they found themselves. The whole context of the passage is practical and there appears to be no serious difficulty in stating that Romans 13.1–7 is part of the extended exhortation which began chapter 12: 'Bless those who persecute you. . . . If possible, so far as it depends upon you, live peaceably with all. . . . Let every person be subject to the governing authorities. . . .'

At this point it seems proper to inquire if by grasping this as the substance of what was being *imparted,* we have sufficiently plumbed the passage as a *communication.* This is particularly important because, on the one hand, everyone can understand what the passage says. There are no curious 'left-overs' or enigmatic phrases. On the whole, this is what we expect of Christians today

---

Philo Judaeus, Practice and Theory, London, 1938. F. C. GRANT (ed.), *Hellenistic Religions*, The Age of Syncretism (Library of Religion 2), New York, 1953. Hugo GRESSMANN, *Die orientalischen Religionen im hellenistisch-römischen Zeitalter*, Berlin and Leipzig, 1930. W. GRUNDMANN, 'δύναμις', *TWNT* II, 1935. Hans JONAS, *The Gnostic Religion:* The Message of the Alien God and the Beginnings of Christianity, Boston, 1958. W. L. KNOX, *Some Hellenistic Elements in Primitive Christianity*, London, 1944. Calvin W. MCEWAN, *The Oriental Origin of Hellenistic Kingship* (Studies in Ancient Oriental Civilization, The Oriental Institute of the University of Chicago, 13), Chicago, 1934. Gilbert MURRAY, *Five Stages of Greek Religion*, Oxford, 1925. M. P. NILSSON, *Greek Piety*, ET, Oxford, 1948; 'Problems of the History of Greek Religion in the Hellenistic and Roman Age', *HTR* 36, 1943, 251–75. A. D. NOCK, 'The Emperor's Divine *Comes*', *Journal of Roman Studies* 37, 1947, 102–16; 'Notes on Ruler-cult, I–IV', *JHS* 48, 1928, 21–43; 'Religious Developments from the Close of the Republic to the Death of Nero', *CAH* X, 465–511; 'The Roman Army and the Religious Year', *HTR* 45, 1952, 187–252; 'Soter and Euergetes', *The Joy of Study*, ed. Sherman E. Johnson, New York, 1951, pp. 127–48. B. REICKE, see p. 17. H. J. ROSE, ' *"Numen inest:"* Animism in Greek and Roman Religion', *HTR* 27, 1935, 237–57. H. SASSE, 'κόσμος', *TWNT* III, 1938. K. L. SCHMIDT, *Die Polis in Kirche und Welt*, Basel, 1939. E. STAUFFER, *Christ and the Caesars*, ET, London, 1955. W. W. TARN, *Hellenistic Civilization*, London, 1927; 'The Hellenistic Ruler-Cult and the Daemon', *JHS* 48, 1928, 206–19. O. WASER, 'Daimon', *Pauly-W*, Bd. IV, 1901.

To the Romans

and there seems nothing unusual in Paul's having written it. Yet on the other hand, having completed the exegesis of the passage, we are faced with some 'theological' problems. What Paul *said* is clear; the problem is rather 'fitting it into his thought'! Precisely because Romans 13.1–7, which seems perfectly understandable, is a problem to practical Christianity today, we must ask if in grasping what Paul had to impart, we really are a party to the *communication*.[1]

At this point, however, the historian would remind us that we are not alone; that Paul was imparting to Rome an exhortation to civil obedience is also the tradition of the Church. No one appears to think anything else was being imparted, except for that hint by Irenaeus that a heretical group had seized on the word *exousiai* to support their cause to the hurt of the Church; i.e., the *exousiai* were identified with the spiritual powers (*Heresies* v 24.1). It is obvious that Irenaeus was not correcting an absurdity—as many have considered the modern thesis. He wrote in earnest. Irenaeus' brief rebuttal is evidence that the concept of *exousiai* as spiritual powers was common enough to be the medium as well as the substance of propagandizing.

Presuming that Irenaeus had a broad knowledge of the Church's tradition and was not withholding honesty for the sake of a better cause, we must value his words. From the Scriptures and traditions of the Church (I Peter 2.13–17; Titus 3.1; *Mart. Polycarp* 10, etc.) it was obvious to him that Paul had nothing to do with the kind of thought fostered by the missionaries of heresy; he had imparted an exhortation with regard to the State and the Christian's relation to it.

The tradition of what Paul was imparting has remained essentially the same, but, while every generation seems to have understood its practical significance, the 'interpretation' of it as well as its

[1] M. S. Enslin ('Light from the Quest', *HTR* 42, 1949, p. 19) quotes an unnamed 'eminent anthropologist': 'When we are probing back into antiquity we need be ever on our guard against the fallacy that what seems to us rational or sensible or practical would have so seemed to them. Thus it has been my experience that when seeking to explain the origin of a practice which still continues, but with no real indication as to what started it, of all the various possible guesses the one which seems to us most 'sensible' or 'reasonable' is the one to be most resolutely excluded. Because a practice so appears to us is no guarantee that it would so have appeared to men under totally different circumstances, whose notion of the world was totally different from our own: in fact, it is usually a guarantee that the exact opposite would be the case.'

'implications' appear to have been problems since relatively early times. Consequently, we must ask again: in grasping what the tradition of the Church affirms to be the substance of this passage —what Paul was *imparting*—do we not yet lack a full share in the *communication*?

The importance of ideas which are inherent in common terms and easier for everyone to translate than to comprehend is apparent in the assertion that the *exousiai* are 'servants of God'. We have no reason to believe that 'God' here would mean to a Graeco-Roman pagan or to an English deist what Paul intended. 'God' was not a strange word in Paul's day. In one sense, everyone knew what it meant, but Paul distinguished his God from the gods and lords who were only demons.[1] Inasmuch as Paul was writing to Christians, however unknown they were, he could and did make certain presumptions,[2] and among them was surely that his readers would understand 'God' in this passage as 'the God and Father of our Lord Jesus Christ'.[3] While the pagan of Paul's time would have had little difficulty in comprehending what Paul was *imparting* in Romans 13, viz., that the readers should be subject to the *exousiai*, would Paul say that the stranger really understood and shared in the *communication* apart from the proper identification of 'God'? No, for the man's obedience would be grounded in the rule of a god who was no god at all, and in his ignorance his whole behaviour would be under the domination of 'elemental spirits' and *daimones*. Consequently it is apparent that the full understanding of what is imparted, what we have been calling participation in communication, depends upon our being of one mind with Paul in a larger sphere. One of the principal difficulties in our exegesis of Romans 13.1–7 lies in the fact that we no longer share the mind of Paul's world in some aspects now forgotten or unappreciated.[4]

---

[1] I Cor. 8.4–6; 10.19 f. Acts 17.22–31 is neither typical of Paul nor wholly opposed to this (cf. Filson, pp. 30 n. 52, and 56 n. 24). Also cf. Rom. 1.21; (16.25 f.;) I Cor. 1.21; 2.6–16; Eph. 2.12; 4.18; Col. 1.21.

[2] E.g. that they had received the Spirit (8.9) and possessed a basic understanding of baptism (6.4) and faith (10.9) (Dibelius, *Paul*, pp. 92–94).

[3] Rom. 15.6. Cf. Filson, pp. 30, 38 f., 54 ff.

[4] A. Schweitzer's criticism of an earlier generation of Pauline scholars (*Paul and His Interpreters*, ET, London, 1912, pp. 37 f.) is to the point here: 'They never call attention to the fact that the Apostle always becomes unintelligible just at the moment when he begins to explain something; never

In this regard, however, we have to account for the fact that the early Church's tradition never emphasized significantly this broader sphere of communication in regard to this passage. Again referring to 'God' in Romans 13, we observe that it is used six times, yet its significance is subordinate to what is being said concerning the *exousiai* and Christian subjection to them. This passage is not a 'theological' statement; we can understand why, when the early Church considered the great passages imparting something concerning God, this one would be omitted. Thus it seems clear, in the first place, that the Scriptures can be indexed only in terms of what they *impart*; that which brings a reader into communication with an ancient writer is beyond the scope of a catalogue. Secondly, there was really no reason why Paul's contemporaries should be consciously concerned with these larger spheres, for the letter to Rome was designed to communicate with them as fellow Christians in the first century, and, like the apostle, they had little interest in writing general, cultural, or religious history. Thus it is that the Church's tradition proves to be an inadequate basis for full participation today in Paul's communication to Rome.

Our problem, however, is essentially with the word *exousiai*. Yet what has been said should make clear our attitude toward this word. Like 'God', *exousiai* was a common word, and it had what a modern scholar would indicate to be more than one shade of meaning in the ancient world. The only thing clearly imparted with regard to the *exousiai* which could be indexed is that they are servants of God, appointed by him to their present work; there appears to have been no necessity of making explicit who they were.[1] Presumably the word *exousiai* was as understandable to the Roman church as was the word 'God', but we have no reason to

---

give a hint that while we hear the sound of his words the tune of his logic escapes us . . . They fail to reckon with the possibility that the original significance of his utterances may rest on presuppositions which are not present to our apprehension and conception. For the same reason they all more or less hold to the opinion that what they have to do with is mainly a psychological problem.'

[1] 'Paul did not work out his theological ideas in great detail, except where his experiences had been so unsettling that they apparently turned his world of traditional ideas upside down', Dibelius, *Paul*, p. 110; cf. Bultmann, *Theology* II, 146 f.

assume that its use in this passage was any less bound to an historical period, or a religious understanding, than the word 'God'. We cannot suppose *a priori* that it has always meant what its use in this passage means to us today. Paul presumed that the Roman saints would understand 'God' because they were Christians; they would understand *exousiai* because they were citizens of the Graeco-Roman world.

The task of understanding Romans 13.1-7 as a communication requires us to consider the significance of the term *exousiai* at the time Paul wrote. This will be done in two sections: (1) The Graeco-Roman conception of the State in the Cosmos. (2) The writer and the readers of the epistle.

THE GRAECO-ROMAN CONCEPTION OF THE STATE IN THE COSMOS

It is the practice of all thorough histories of antiquity to concern themselves with the theory of government and the cosmology of particular peoples and periods. The usual practice, however, is to separate these two concerns. While this is convenient for the editor and enables the writer to concentrate upon things one at a time, the end result can be artificial and create a false impression. As will be seen below, the average citizen of the Graeco-Roman world did not divide his thought, feeling, and experiences into 'chapters'. While ancient writers could discourse at length upon single aspects of a complexity, the religious life and hope of the masses was not so easily isolated from other affairs. The academic practice of breaking down complex relationships for research must not be allowed to dominate our understanding of the actual living situation of the people.

Systematic lexicography has followed the academic pattern by making the observation that the word *exousiai* has two uses: one referring to civil magistrates, the other to spiritual powers. While this makes writing and use of a lexicon much simpler, it yet runs the risk of artificiality and leads men to conclude that the ancients customarily engaged in purely mythological speculations on the one hand, or dealt strictly with sober historical facts on the other, without any danger of 'confusing' the two. The logic of systematic modern scholarship has lured exegetes into forcing the same kind of logic upon the ancient mind. Since the word *exousiai* appears in the paragraph on civil government as well as that on cosmology, we have been too quick to ask ourselves: Which meaning does this particular usage indicate? To choose either might do violence to the ancient mind, while to say 'both' is not only to confuse our present thought but to indicate that the ancient made a dual or ambiguous reference. It is quite possible that the idea was a unity. In considering 'the State in the Cosmos' we hope to allow any relationship which may have existed between the 'two' spheres in the ancient mind to be recognized without any artificial separation or blending of them.[1]

The State and the Hellenistic Spirit

The key word, at least the one most commonly used, for the Hellenistic period is *syncretism*.[2] It does not suffice to explain causes, identify origins, or make much more known about the age than that it was composite, a mixture rather than a compound. Lacking any real unity of cultural tradition or religious heritage, the peoples of this period shared in the new and growing *universalism* which appears to have revealed the inadequacy of older nationalistic and cultural limitations of that period. *Individualism*[3] became the pattern, for men were seeking something spiritually as well as intellectually satisfying.

They took no part in political life, they knew nothing of patriotism, they were uprooted, emigrated to foreign countries or were born there, they mingled with the natives and with people from many countries, and mixed marriages were numerous. They had broken the bonds by which the family and the city-state held men together, they were

---

[1] A. J. Festugière, *Le Dieu Cosmique* (*La Révélation d'Hermès Trismégiste*, Vol. II, Paris, 1949), shows clearly how well rooted is this approach in ancient philosophy; and he follows its development into the period of special interest to us. Until Strobel's study, 'Zum Verständnis von Röm. 13', (see p. 40) which appears to recognize the significance of the secular context of Paul's communication, opponents of the new exegesis of Rom. 13. 1-7 have based their argument from classical authors upon Harald Fuch's study, *Der geistige Widerstand gegen Rom in der antiken Welt*, n. 71, pp. 58 f. But both Strobel and Fuchs, like others in the debate (cf. pp. 57 f. above), relied heavily upon indexes and lexicons and fell short of entering into the communication.

[2] Gressmann, p. 10; Grant, Introduction; Andres, p. 300 (1 ff.).

[3] Individualism was the 'dominant feature of the age ... not so much from the greatness of individuals as from the weakness of society' (Ferguson, p. 4). Men were 'no longer a part of anything *except the universe*' (Jonas, p. 247).

thrown back on themselves. They were able to choose their companions as they liked among men as well as among gods. They turned in a direction in which they believed they would find refuge and consolation. Identity of ideas and interests, not family and state, determined their associations.[1]

It was the great alteration of civil life which appears to underlie the radical change in the outlook of the common man in the new world. This is particularly true with regard to his conception of of the State in the Cosmos. Compared to the traffic in ideas and superstitions which flowed over the broken barriers of nation and tongue in the Hellenistic period, the earlier international influences in philosophy and science were of relatively little importance, for they were eventually assimilated to the Greek mind.[2] The change which was realized in Hellenistic thought with regard to the State in the Cosmos (as with so much else) did not grow out of a vacuum nor out of an undisturbed reflection upon the gods or a speculation about one's fortune in an animate natural world, but out of the real and amazing transformation in the character of the political and social world. It was on the whole the radical development in the form and nature of the State which demanded a rethinking, not only of local and state political theory, but also, quite naturally for the ancient mind, although it may seem strange to us, of the character of the Cosmos.[3]

The Background of the Graeco-Roman Concept of the State in the Cosmos

The Near Eastern background.[4]—It is valuable first of all to observe that consideration of the effect of political change upon man's understanding of the world in which he lives touches upon ways of thought deeply rooted in the ancient world; they were not a

---

[1]Nilsson, 'Problems', p. 261; cf. Tarn, *Hel. Civ.*, pp. 268 f.; Schmidt, *Polis*, pp. 97–107.
[2]Nilsson, *Greek Piety*, p. 190.
[3]Cf. Barker's distinction between political theory (self-conscious speculation by individuals) and political thought ('the thought of a whole society and not necessarily or often self-conscious'), p. 505.
[4]This section draws esp. on the work of the following in their respective fields: H. and H. A. Frankfort, 'The Emancipation of Thought from Myth' and 'Myth and Reality', *IAAM*, pp. 363–88, 3–27; *Kingship and the Gods*; O. R. Gurney, *The Hittites*, London, 1952; Thorkild Jacobsen, 'Mesopotamia', *IAAM*, pp. 123–220; John A. Wilson, 'Egypt', *IAAM*, pp. 29–122.

new or Hellenistic creation. In the ancient East, cosmology was as closely related to the affairs of state as to the cycles of nature, and the correlation between nature and human activity was the basis for their 'mythopoeic thought'.[1] This relationship is evident in the Egyptian and Mesopotamian conception of the State and accounts for the basic differences in thought between the two countries.

In Egypt the lordly reign of the sun and the regularity of the life-giving Nile floods seemed to declare a world order in which Egypt was central and the people were assured of life's recurring triumph over death. Change was 'either superficial and insignificant or an unfolding in time of what had been pre-ordained from the beginning'.[2] In this context kingship, the rule of the pharaoh, the son and image of the Creator, was the guarantee of social stability through the integration of nature and society in an abiding harmony. In monophysite Egyptian thought the divinity of the king was specifically set forth for political purposes. The cosmological definition of the king's political significance is particularly evident in his titles: 'the pharaoh was made Son of Re for the specific purpose of ruling Re's chief concern, the land of Egypt.'[3] He was 'Lord of the two Lands' because 'it was a function of government to make Upper and Lower Egypt an effective single nation'.[4] Thus the 'Two Lords', Horus and Seth, were united in the person of the king. As the falcon Horus, the pharaoh held 'divine credentials to rule in the palace as the god who had been awarded the kingship by the divine tribunal.'[5] As the *ka*, the twin and guardian spirit of each individual, the king played a strong spiritual role in the life and order of his country.

To the Mesopotamian, by contrast, 'cosmic *order* did not appear as something given; rather it became something achieved';[6] society had no guaranteed stability in this land of the thunderstorm, where men dwelt in anxiety under great natural powers. There the human State was but a secondary form within the cosmic State, presided over by a divine assembly which

[1] *IAAM, passim;* Frankfort, *Kingship,* pp. 3–12, 61 f. n. 4; McEwan, p. 3.
[2] Frankfort, 'Emancipation', p. 366; cf. *Kingship,* pp. 4 f.
[3] Wilson, p. 71; cf. McEwan, pp. 6–8; Frankfort, *Kingship,* pp. 159–61.
[4] Wilson, pp. 73 f.
[5] *Ibid.,* p. 75.
[6] Jacobsen, p. 127.

The Powers That Be

appointed mortals to rulership on earth. But that ruler remained subject to their favour, and not even a king was assured security.

Hence the king and his counsellors watched for portents on earth and in the sky which might reveal a changing constellation of divine grace, so that the catastrophe might be foreseen and possibly averted. In Egypt neither astrology nor prophecy ever developed to any great extent.[1]

The Mesopotamian cosmology was far more influential upon its contemporaries than the Egyptian,[2] and the similarity between the old Mesopotamian divine assembly and our earlier discussion of folk angels is apparent. In the Mesopotamian *Weltanschauung* the assembly of gods chose one of its members, a god, to assume active leadership with the authority of Anu and the executive power of Enlil. This deity fulfilled this function among the gods, but upon earth he acted through his human steward, the ruler of the god's city-state. Obviously the whole cosmic structure not only grew out of a view of nature, but had definite correspondence to observable political events. A change in the supremacy of the city-states called for a new understanding of the divine assembly's actions. An earthly king was deposed in favour of another because the divine assembly had voted in a new government. The wide acceptance of this understanding is evident in the Assyrian adaptation of the Akkadian myth *Enuma elish* by substituting the victorious Assur in the place of Marduk, who had been supreme among the gods in the days of Babylon's rule.

While political events did not create cosmological systems, they appear to have played an active part in the definition and development of them. Whether it is the Son of Re as the embodiment of Horus and Seth, or the presiding god in the divine assembly as the patron of the ruling king, the affairs of state were affairs of the Cosmos.[3]

Another pre-Hellenistic oriental culture can further illustrate our observations. The Hittite state, which, like the Mesopotamian, developed kingship from an earlier rule by nobles, followed a

[1] Frankfort, 'Emancipation', p. 366; cf. *Kingship*, p. 248.
[2] Wilson, p. 119; Jacobsen, p. 126.
[3] Cf. Frankfort, *Kingship*, *passim*, e.g. pp. 32 f., 102, 231 f., 277 ff., 309. McEwan finds this common to the Orient and discusses briefly Assyrian and Persian aspects (pp. 8, 12 ff.). Cf. p. 78 n. 1 below.

familiar process. Organization of isolated communities for civil and military reasons involved many local councils and cults. While considerable independence was allowed, effective centralization of government required the support of the constituent communities, and this is preserved in the lists of local gods who confirmed important state documents. The ingenuity of bureaucracy brought about a classification of the various local gods according to their similarity, and by identification steps were made toward a pantheon. The most characteristic of Hittite deities was the weather-god. While he shared the rule of the Heavens with the imported sun-goddess, he alone represented the State in international affairs. It is characteristic of Near Eastern thought that a treaty between Hattusilis III and Ramesses II of Egypt was made for the purpose of 'making eternal the relations which the Sun-god of Egypt and the Weather-god of Hatti have established for the land of Egypt and the land of Hatti'.[1] It is understandable that the government and the nation's temple buildings should be identical, for affairs of state were part of the divine order of the Cosmos.

The Greek background.—When we see how little of the great cultural tradition of Greece was inherited by Hellenistic religion, we see the ground for Gilbert Murray's statement that the Hellenistic age inherited a '*tabula rasa*'.[2] Traditional Greek religion had acquired significance for the State by analogy to its place in the religion of the family. Consequently there was no official priesthood, but religion was observed as a part of community life. 'Piety towards the gods bound the members of clan and State together in conscious union in relation to the higher powers.'[3] With this firm association between gods and the State, Greek religion was yet an interesting deviation from the oriental pattern noted above, in which alterations in earthly rule were reflected in the government of the Cosmos, for the Homeric description of a

[1] Gurney, p. 140.
[2] Murray, pp. 158 f. Although granting that the specifically religious concepts of the period were indebted to the Orient, Jonas (*passim*) emphasizes the role of philosophical universals in the characteristic thought of the period. It was the oriental heritage, however, which aided the popularization of philosophical universals and for the first time made them influential in common religious life.
[3] Nilsson, *Greek Piety*, p. 8.

The Powers That Be

divine monarchy had been so deeply impressed upon the Greek mind that it survived the overthrow of kingship. 'Earth might be republican, but heaven remained a monarchy.'[1] While Themistocles, after the battles at Salamis and Plataea, could declare, 'It is not we who have done this, but the gods and heroes,'[2] the picture is less like the oriental view than the words would seem to indicate. The centre of gravity in the ancient Greek world was not the Olympian council of Zeus, but the *polis*. The devout ascription of victory to the gods and heroes was based upon their participation in battle alongside the Greeks; it was no thanksgiving for heavenly legislation or even heavenly warfare. After the Persians were defeated the bond between the State and religion was celebrated in splendid monuments to the gods. That point of little distinction where heroes are defined as gods[3] was reached again; gods increasingly were defined as heroes.[4] The identification of the gods with the *polis* was so close that a modern scholar could conclude, 'If a good Greek had his *polis*, he had an adequate substitute in most respects for any mythological gods.'[5] It was this emphasis upon the *polis* which proved so drastically vulnerable to the new and larger world of the Hellenistic period. When the new science proved that the earth was at the heart of a vast universe, the *polis* theology was found inadequate, and a decided advantage was given to the oriental religions whose cosmology was far more easily adapted to universal dimensions. The Greeks, who had made their gods an appendage to their *polis*, found the new universe too large a tail for so small a dog to wag. The Graeco-Roman conception of the State in the Cosmos would have to be built upon oriental tradition, for the heritage of Greece was at a loss to cope with the new world.

[1] Nilsson, *Greek Piety*, p. 3.
[2] Herodotus VIII 109.
[3] Cf. Waser, p. 2011 (27 ff.); Knox, p. 39; Nock, 'Ruler-Cult', p. 37 and its n. 85.
[4] Nock cites Attalus III on the honouring of Zeus Sabazios, ' "whom, as he was our comrade and helper in many deeds and many dangers, we decided because of his manifestations of divine power to enshrine in a temple of Athena Nicephorus. This we thought would be a place suitable and worthy of him." This god, like an earthly ruler, is thus given the position of *synnaos theos* in a temple possessing prestige, as a recognition of services rendered' ('Divine *Comes*', p. 102; cf. another example, p. 103 n. 13. The text: Dittenberger, *Orientis Graeci Inscriptiones*, Leipzig, 1903, No. 331 [51 ff.]).
[5] Murray, p. 159; cf. Nock, 'Ruler-Cult', p. 31.

To the Romans

Main Currents in the Graeco-Roman Period

The range of that movement called Hellenism is too broad to be reviewed here. We must confine ourselves to those aspects which help us understand the place of the State in the Cosmos for men of that time. Since we cannot divide our subject horizontally, State and Cosmos, we will divide it vertically to consider four aspects of Hellenistic thought which transect State and Cosmos and will illuminate our concern: Power, Astrology, Monotheism, *Daimones*.

Power in the Graeco-Roman period.—Man's concern with power in the world is as old as religious thought, but this idea achieved a new significance in the Hellenistic period, not merely among those who could yet be classed as 'primitive', but with men of learning, e.g., Posidonius and Philo. Concern with power 'is a fundamental factor in the idea which late antiquity held of the world and nature, and also in the religious innovations, and forms the most marked difference between the earlier and later religion of Greece'.[1] The earlier philosophical union of world principle and deity to produce a neutral kind of divinity took on personality and colour in its contact with pagan religion. The various gods were associated with the δυνάμεις of the Omnipotent as personifications of his powers.[2] The systematization of this process was the work of Posidonius, whose philosophical assimilation of the oriental spirit was instrumental in the transition to Hellenism.[3] The main feature of this development was the subjection of the Cosmos to the guardianship of powers.[4] Their mysteriousness was no longer to be dissipated by the concept of a cosmic order, but the Cosmos itself was absorbed by the mystery surrounding the powers which occupied human thought more and more as the deity withdrew to the borders of an expanding Cosmos; 'The world is a manifestation (*Erscheinung*) of the powers working in

---

[1] Nilsson, *Greek Piety*, p. 108.
[2] Grundmann, p. 289 (1 ff.). Cf. Diogenes Laertius II 305.15 ff. and Plutarch, *De Iside et Osiride* 67 (ii. 377 f.) where the Demiurge (Logos, guardian Providence) presides over the Cosmos but rules through his powers which have been *appointed* over all things (texts in Grundmann, p. 289 [40–44, 49–51]).
[3] Grundmann, pp. 287 (40 ff.), 289 (1–12), 289 (54)–290 (13); Nilsson, *Greek Piety*, pp. 103, 106; Jonas, p. 19.
[4] Cf. *PGM*, IV, 1275 f.; 1331.

her, through her, and upon her.'[1] In order to be effective one must know and co-operate with these 'world rulers'. In the higher religions the power concept served to explain the relationship between deity and the facts of world history and human destiny, but in the lower religions the belief in powers became the basis for the popular and growing belief in *daimones*, magic, amulets, etc.[2] And in this animate Cosmos, where the wills of men were inferior as well as in the minority, it is not surprising that there should result what a modern scholar would consider a confounding of the natural world with the spiritual, a confusion of myth and history, a mixture of superstition and faith, of magic and religion. The ability of simple folk to disassociate a symbol from the power behind it was no greater in antiquity than today, when statues and medals enjoy a popular use beyond the bounds of the theology which sanctions them. Nilsson has cited Moschopoulos, a Byzantine author, who assessed the situation well.

You must know that the pagans (Hellenes, pagan Greeks) supposed that all that they saw possessed of power could not exercise that power without the superintendence of gods, and they called that which was possessed of power and its superintendent deity by the same name. Hence they used 'Hephaistos' to mean the fire which serves us and the superintendent of the acts which are active by means of fire.[3]

It is this broad and popular concept of power in the Graeco-Roman period upon which a number of the most characteristic beliefs of that age depend. Not only in general, but also in great detail the world was considered subject to the guardianship and authority of gods, spirits, and *daimones*; formulas, symbols, and special objects were treasured for their actual ability to influence these 'world rulers' and 'elemental spirits' with regard to the health, prosperity, and social relationships of men who used them properly, and we cannot suppose that symbols and physical

---

[1] Grundmann, p. 290 (8 f.) after K. Reinhardt.
[2] Cf. Goodenough, *Jewish Symbols*, II, 159 f.; Nilsson, 'Problems', p. 264; *Greek Piety*, pp. 108 f. 'We make a distinction between occultism and spiritism on the one hand, magic and sorcery on the other . . . This distinction is not valid for late antiquity' (*ibid.*, pp. 145 f.; cf. Nock, 'Divine *Comes*', p. 104).
[3] Nilsson, *Greek Piety*, p. 106 (from Introd. to scholia on Hesiod, *Works and Days* [Jacoby, *Fragmente der griechischen Historiker*, fragments 244 and 352 of Apollodorus]).

objects were always consciously distinguished from the invisible powers associated with them. It is precisely the dynamic character of the Hellenistic world which renders the vocabulary of that period so complex for us today; our modern effort to analyse words used in magical formulas and power concepts as *either* fact *or* fancy appears to be wholly unrealistic.[1]

Astrology in the Graeco-Roman period.—'Astrology fell upon the Hellenistic mind as a new disease falls upon some remote island people;'[2] its influence was thorough enough to include our concern with the State in the Cosmos. While the Greeks eventually surpassed the Orientals in astronomy, it is not their scientific progress which concerns us, because it was not associated with religion or human destiny in the minds of the people. It was astrology from the East which filled in the gap left by an expanding universe and a static Greek religion. The fact that Babylon was the first to establish a scientific cosmic religion, broad enough to encompass world conquerors as well as displaced populations under the universal astral deities, played an important part in the appeal of oriental religions to a world which had burst the bonds of national religions and sought a more comprehensive and satisfying faith.[3] From the beginning astrology belonged to the religious elements which were to characterize Hellenistic thought, and no popular movement was to escape its influence.[4] 'Astrology revolutionized the world in which lived men with no tincture of philosophy by bringing them for the first time in touch with universals.'[5]

The basis for astrology is the older belief in a correspondence between the activities of the gods above and events of human history below. Earlier we observed that this concept was integral to ancient oriental thought, and now we see that *astrology built upon this ancient concept of correspondence which had its origin in the idea*

---

[1]Cf. Grundmann, p. 289 (14–16, 37 ff.): The relatively sparse use of the word 'power' as compared with *daimon* or the many names may be attributed to its colourless and impersonal neutrality. But the idea of power underlies many other terms more personal or specific.

[2]Murray, p. 177.

[3]Cumont, *Astrology*, pp. 14 f.

[4]*Ibid.*, pp. xxiv, 81, 90; Nilsson, *Greek Piety*, p. 113.

[5]Nock, 'Relig. Develop.', p. 505. Cf. also Angus, ch. XV, 'Astral Religion and its Catholic Appeal'; Festugière, Part I, ch. V, paragraph 1.

*of the place of the State in the Cosmos.*¹ And the vast scale of political activity in the Graeco-Roman period is a significant context for the spread of this idea.²

Astrology spread far and wide, and became an integral part of the popular conception of the world, because it offered men the possibility of making sense of an environment which did not make sense by itself.³ It was doubtless the desire of the Stoic philosophy to comprehend the new world, and to present its bewildered citizens with a satisfying way of life, which made both Zeno and Posidonius receptive to astrology.⁴ On the one hand astrology strengthened the argument of those who opposed the widespread belief in the rule of Tyche, the goddess of Fortune. The Stoic was given a scientific basis for setting forth the doctrine of a united and harmonious universe; it was not Chance which ruled but divine Providence. But on the other hand the astrological proof was rigid and the philosophic mind drew the conclusion that the real lord of a mechanical cosmic system was Fate. However, 'this side of astrology was over the heads of ordinary folk.'⁵ From the hopeful aspect of astrology they concluded that there was some kind of order and established authority in the Cosmos. Through divination they sought to discover what lay in the future for them; by means of magic they hoped to alter or improve it; with amulets and other symbols they hoped to acquire and maintain the favour of the powers which reigned over them. On the grimmer side of astrology it was the avowed intention of certain popular movements of the period to help their members to break through the determined, and therefore oppressive and evil, rule implied by the course of the stars. The chief means for escaping Fate were *gnosis*, magic, and mystery religions.⁶

---

¹Cumont observes: 'The development of the old Babylonian religion bears no relation to astronomical theories. It was rather the political circumstances which gave to certain gods in turn the primacy among the multitude of divinities worshipped in the land of Sumer and Accad, and . . . caused the functions of other local powers to be attributed to their all-usurping and all-absorbing personality' (*Astrology*, p. 22; cf. Festugière, pp. 89–91, esp. p. 90 n. 1).

²'Princes who proclaimed themselves rulers of the world could not be protected save by cosmopolitan gods' (Cumont, *Astrology*, p. 55).

³Sasse, p. 879 (2–27).

⁴Cumont, *Astrology*, pp. 69 f., 83 f.; cf. Andres, p. 297 (58 ff.).

⁵Nilsson, *Greek Piety*, p. 111.

⁶Tarn, *Hel. Civ.*, pp. 290 f.; Nilsson, *Greek Piety*, p. 112; Jonas, pp. 254–65.

To the Romans

It was the belief in correspondence and order dominated by heavenly powers which was of particular significance with regard to the Graeco-Roman conception of the State in the Cosmos. E. R. Goodenough has examined several Pythagorean fragments dating from the Hellenistic period and suggests that they offer a key to the 'official political philosophy of the Hellenistic age'.[1] While the structure of the texts is generally that of parallel and analogy, it is evident that the State is conceived to be within a universal divine order in which the king occupies a unique position as an earthly instrument for universal harmony.[2] If this Pythagorean conception represents the '*official* political philosophy', we have no assurance that it was everywhere observed on so high a plane. If the common man did not speculate about the correspondence between king and god, world and state, in the same terms as the philosophers, we should not be surprised. On the other hand, it would be unwarranted to suggest that his views were not more nearly like those of his contemporaries, however learned, than our own. As the empire was world-wide, politics was of universal dimensions and belonged to the order of things. The individual's concern for civil peace and justice was not so different from his hope for the favourable disposition of the seasons and for good health. While a Pythagorean could say that the king is to the world (empire) as God is to the universe, and that he is a deity among men[3] or, in the more cautious words of Plutarch, 'Rulers are ministers of God for the care and safety of mankind, that they may distribute or hold in safe keeping the blessings and benefits which God gives to men,'[4] to the unlearned

---

We will make no particular study of the mystery religions, as they were rather the reflection of the movements which we are considering than a vital force in themselves (Nilsson, *Greek Piety*, p. 161; 'Problems', pp. 269 f.).

[1] Goodenough, 'Hellenistic Kingship', pp. 102, 57. Nock relates this type of political theory to the concept of the ruler's *daimon*: 'According to this, the ruler is an earthly counterpart of divinity, and this divinity is commonly conceived as solar' ('Divine *Comes*', p. 114). Cf. Cumont, *Astrology*, pp. 87 f.; Bréhier, p. 23; Goodenough, *Politics of Philo*, pp. 94 ff.

[2] Cf. Ecphantus in Stob. I 6.19; IV 7.65; Goodenough, 'Hellenistic Kingship', pp. 84, 90.

[3] Cf. the first fragment *On Kingship* by Diotogenes (Stob. IV 7.61) cited by Goodenough, 'Hellenistic Kingship', p. 68; cf. Bréhier, p. 19 f.

[4] Plutarch, *Princip. Inerud.* v 13.22–14.2 (Goodenough, 'Hellenistic Kingship', p. 95). Cf. Andres, pp. 301 (42)–305 (62): Plutarch accepted a view in

man the universal rulers, emperor and powers, appeared to have more in common than they had differences.[1] The seat of imperial authority was so far removed that it belonged to the universal order. How the emperor, as a deputy in that system, compared with other beings appointed to authority and invested with power, could have been merely an academic matter.

It has been important for us to consider the place of astrology in Graeco-Roman thought because: (1) It was one of the most significant characteristics of thought in this period, with a wide cultural, intellectual, and religious appeal. (2) It was based upon, and became the medium for the propagation of, the idea of correspondence in a united cosmic order. Here it became closely integrated with the idea of power, discussed above, and a coherent *Weltanschauung* became possible. (3) There is strong evidence that an important political philosophy and a wide range of popular thought associated the world empire and cosmic order after the pattern of the older oriental theory discussed above. (4) Astrological interest in universal harmony permeated the cosmic context within which politics and the emperor were viewed, and belief in rulers as 'ministers of God for the care and safety of mankind' was only natural to men for whom 'world rulers', spiritual and civil, were instruments of divine Providence.

In short, astrology, as a principal factor in Graeco-Roman thought, was of decisive significance in giving a cosmic dimension to affairs of state in the thought of that period. This is not to say that men could not think of kings or government without thinking of stars, but that astrology had so accustomed men to think in terms of cosmic unity and correspondence that the world State and its ruler were quite naturally assumed to be a part of the universal order.

Monotheism in the Graeco-Roman period.—As has been evident

---

which *daimones* presided over whole lands (*De Fort. Rom.* II, *Demosth.* 19), p. 303 (33 ff.). He also recorded that Caesar's guardian *daimon* was mightier than Pompey's (*Caes.* 69, cf. *Cat.* 54). This compares very closely with what has been considered the *Jewish* conception of folk angels. Demonology was important for Plutarch as a means of understanding the order of the world (p. 305 [36]). Cf. Glover, pp. 153–67.

[1] Cf. W. Michaelis, 'κοσμοκράτωρ, παντακράτωρ', *TWNT* III, 913 f.; cf. Frankfort, *Kingship*, pp. 309, 311 f., for a similar situation in Mesopotamia.

To the Romans

already, an important phase in the development of Graeco-Roman religious thought has been the tendency toward monotheism. There were several forces at work simultaneously. Some sort of integration of the great numbers of gods which flooded the ancient world was a necessity if the gods were to have any meaning or prove worthy of religious devotion. As noted above, harmonization was an early aspect of this development; gods were arranged according to type.[1] It was the tendency of syncretism to strip the host of deities of their individuality, and there developed a sense of 'Pantheos' (*Allgott*) which was not exclusive, i.e., Sarapis was recognized as universal god as well as Isis.[2] The tendency toward monotheism never completely eliminated polytheism, but it was successful to the extent that it had both popular and intellectual appeal. The place of astrology in this development is generally recognized,[3] and the cosmological approach was one of the most effective arguments for the unity of the universe under a single supreme god.[4] The Stoics aided the movement in their arguments for an integrated universe.[5]

Godhead was one; there were many telephone lines and they ran through a number, smaller but appreciable, of switchboards. You used one or another according to what seemed appropriate for a particular purpose or place; a *comes* gave you the equivalent of a private line.[6]

As indicated above, the popular concept of the universe's subjection to the vassals of one god was in terms of the powers. This form of monotheism was encouraged by a contemporary science 'which made *no distinction between physical and occult forces* . . . the latter being the more important.'[7] In mentioning the various forces which worked in the direction of a 'general cosmological religion for the whole world',[8] we must not forget that it was not chiefly through inquiry and deduction or disinterested speculation but from the conscious need of the Graeco-Roman populace that the bulk of the religious thought we are considering developed.

[1] Cf. Ferguson, p 5; Andres, p. 300.
[2] Gressmann, p. 10.
[3] Angus, p. 258.
[4] Nilsson, *Greek Piety*, pp. 120 f.
[5] Tarn, *Hel. Civ.*, p. 280.
[6] Nock, 'Divine *Comes*', p. 104.
[7] Nilsson, 'Problems', p. 264. Italics are mine.
[8] Nilsson, *Greek Piety*, p. 121.

The power of the popular mind is too easily unappreciated because it was not literary. Yet we may observe that Zeno and Epicurus, both uncompromising thinkers who constructed complete philosophical systems almost free from popular superstitions, finally admitted the spiritual powers because the consensus supported belief in them.[1]

It is evident that, while we have discussed power, astrology, and monotheism in separate paragraphs, they are closely interwoven, especially in the ordinary thought of our period. These concepts were actually part of a *total* view of the ancient world. As the physical and occult forces blended and religion was hardly distinguishable from magic in this period, the documents of learned ancients upon whom we must depend should not lead us to consider the place of the State in that ancient world as any less a part of its dynamic and vital unity. While astrology's emphasis upon correspondence between heaven and earth served to draw the State into an integrated universe, the monotheistic character of that order was no less directly derived from the contemporary political system.

It is beyond doubt that the monarchical government of the State, which had been the prevailing form since the Hellenistic period began, and particularly since the Roman Empire became a really world-wide domination, contributed largely to promote monotheism. For the world of the gods is everywhere, in pagan religion, modelled after the constitution of the State. . . . The monarchical and well-organized form of the State under the Emperors made the idea appear natural that the universe was controlled by a supreme Governor enthroned in the heavens.[2]

Again we see that the State not only existed in the Cosmos, but played a decisive part in understanding the character of the universe.[3] As will be obvious below, the emperor, whatever the stage of his 'divinity', was always held in common thought in a context including other powers at a time when these gods were increasingly thought to be subordinate to a universal omnipotent Ruler. He was a world ruler, and as such had a significant part in

[1] Murray, pp. 161 f.; Andres, pp. 290 (14 ff.).
[2] Nilsson, *Greek Piety*, p. 121. Cf. Nock, 'Soter', p. 146.
[3] 'The Myth of the Empire' comprehended 'the whole of history, in nature and in humanity, in heaven and on earth . . . as the history of the Empire' (Stauffer, pp. 21 f.).

the universal order which included a variety of special powers and rulers.

The tendency toward monotheism is important for us in two ways: (1) It was stimulated by the world-wide aspect of imperial rule. (2) It considered the State to be part of a cosmic order and its ruler to be a power whose authority was derived from and part of the rule of one divinity.

The concept of daimones *in the Graeco-Roman period.*—The Graeco-Roman belief in *daimones* was not of the same character as the movements just described. This belief rose from primitive folk-religion to add colour to the impersonal abstract reflection of philosophy regarding intermediary beings,[1] and it responded to the influx of eastern influences as a hidden flavour to a pinch of salt. *Daimon* indicated a superhuman, generally divine being,[2] frequently related to man in one way or other as his guardian (*genius, comes*), as a force affecting his destiny directly or indirectly, or even as the 'divine part' of a man.[3]

In the idea of the *daimon* we see a convergence of the great themes, power, astrology, and monotheism. It is in this conception of the spiritual deputies of the one great God who are entrusted with the government of the world that several particular words gained their meaning: 'principalities, rulers, powers, authorities, thrones, world rulers, dominions, elemental spirits'. It was from their domination that the gnostic, mystery,

[1] In Plato the *daimon* was a 'supernatural element incidentally impinging upon life'. This 'generic term for divine intermediaries between gods and men' combined with the aspect of a guardian angel and a divine element within man, so that the '*daimon* is now linked to the individual by a permanent and not an incidental relationship' (Nock, 'Divine *Comes*,' p. 109). Cf. Nilsson, 'Problems', p. 263; Rose, '*Numen*', pp. 243–9. On the history of the development of the concept, cf. W. Foerster, 'δαίμων', *TWNT* II, 1 ff.; A. C. Pearson, 'Demons and Spirits (Greek)', *ERE* IV, 590–4; Andres, p. 267 (45) ff.: on the *daimon* in folk belief pp. 269–79; in the Hellenistic period, p. 300.

[2] Cf. Liddell-S: In distinction to 'god', *daimon* more frequently indicated 'the Divine power'; Waser, pp. 2010 (26 ff.), 2011 (33 ff.). Cf. Plutarch's citation of Menander: 'By each man standeth from his natal hour/ A *daimon*, his kind mystagogue through life' (Glover, p. 163).

[3] Cf. Waser, p. 2010 (39 ff.), 64 ff.); Andres, pp. 287 (52 ff.), 299 (23 ff.). In *CH* the 'persecuting *daimones*' serve a purpose not unlike the wrath of God in Rom. 1.18 ff., cf. I Cor. 5.5. Cf. *CH* IX 5; XVI 13–16; *Asclep.* 25; *PGM* VII, 303; Plotinus IV 8.5 (22–24); Nock-F, p. 102 n. 10 (F), p. 212 n. 39 (F); Dodd, p. 171 n. 2.

The Powers That Be

and magic movements strove to liberate their adherents.[1]

The philosophers meanwhile found it difficult to reconcile the evil in history with the administration of good *daimones* (the only kind which a wise god would place in charge). Porphyry, in trying to solve this ethical problem, reveals more of the world view of the Graeco-Roman period.[2] His cosmology is comparable to that of the Hermetica:[3] the supreme God, the astral deities, the *daimones*, men, each under the authority of the preceding ruler and all under the one God. It is through this chain of command that one is related to God (*CH* I 24–26). Besides the good *daimones*, which preside not only over men but over the seasons, arts, learning, medicine, etc., and which can do no evil, there are the evil *daimones* which have no official appointment and compensate for it by trying to usurp authority, attract worship to themselves, and degrade the great gods.[4] Throughout, Porphyry appears to be arguing against a popular and prevailing[5] notion that both good and evil flow from the one set of *daimones* appointed by the great God. It seems obvious that his thesis is essentially a refinement of a long accepted conception of divine government.[6]

This same process was being carried out in Christian thought, as is evident from the writing of Origen against Celsus.[7] Following the tradition of the Church from Paul's time, Origen does not deny the existence of *daimones*, but like the pagan philosophers he was faced with a contradiction which had to be put straight. It was not only ethical, but concerned the religious aspects of cosmology. His opponent, Celsus, appears to have held the well-

---

[1] Cf. *CH* I 9, 23, 24–26; VI 1, 3; VIII 4; IX 3; X 7; XVI 5, 13 ff.; Nock-F, p. 20 n. 27 (C), p. 24 n. 57 (F, C), p. 102 n. 11 (C), p. 187 n. 18 (F), p. 212 n. 37 (F, C).

[2] *Abst.* III 37–43. Marcion's solution was more simple but more radical: the pre-Christian Cosmocrator was not good. On good and evil *daimones*, cf. Waser, p. 2010 (26 ff.); Andres, p. 289 (6 ff.).

[3] Cf. *CH* XVI 13 ff., summarized in XVI 18; Scott, II, 429 f.

[4] Cf. *CH* XVI 13 f. As a whole *CH* is not so expressly clear with regard to the problem of evil as Porphyry. Cf. *CH* I 26a and X 7, 19a. Cf. Nock-F, appendix B (pp. 138–40 F, N); cf. p. 102 n. 10 (F), n. 11 (C).

[5] *Abst.* III 40.

[6] Cf. Iamblichus V, 14; Stob., *Herm. Exc.* VI 10; Nock-F, appendix C (pp. 140–2).

[7] Cf. Andres, p. 310 (12 ff.) for the similarities between Celsus' views on *daimones* and those of Plutarch. Cf. above p. 79, and n. 3. On the use in patristic literature, see E. C. E. Owen, 'Δαίμων and Cognate Words', *Journal of Theological Studies* 32, 1931, pp. 133–53.

To the Romans

established views of his time: in a basically monotheistic order of the universe many gods were subordinated with set authorities.[1] Consequently, whatever one does upon earth unavoidably involves *daimones*, for they are responsible for all we eat, drink, and breathe.[2] In an unsophisticated reliance upon the accepted view of things Celsus is easily involved in the contradiction which later philosophers were interested in correcting; the *daimones* appear to be authors of both the good and the evil.[3] Of specific importance is Celsus' view that the *daimones* were instrumental in the appointment of rulers.[4] This association of the rulers and *daimones* was part of the order of things, basic to a citizen's attitude toward his ruler and the whole civil government. It is from this connexion that the refusal of Christians to worship *daimones* subjected them to charges of both atheism and sedition.[5]

Considering the unwillingness of Origen to compromise with Celsus or to place any emphasis upon their agreements, the church Father shows a striking dependence upon the ancient view of 'world rulers', which the Christian Church inherited to a great extent by way of Judaism's previous adaptation.[6] Origen does not 'demythologize', but agrees that the rule of the world is 'only in consequence of the agency and control of certain beings whom we may call invisible husbandmen and guardians', although he insists that they are not *daimones* (VIII 31). Rather, he assigns the subordinate guardianship and rule of the earth to angels.[7] In this

---

[1] *Celsus* VII 68, 70; VIII 2, 33, 58, 65. In V 25 Celsus holds to a system very similar to Jewish folk angel belief.

[2] VIII 31. Cf. Philipp Merlan, 'Celsus', *RAC* II, 956. Merlan observes that the ruler and the demons are competitors because VIII 28 attributes to *daimones* what VIII 67 states has been committed to the ruler. For modern men this is a contradiction, but not for Celsus; universal government was considered something entrusted to subordinates by the supreme God (cf. VII 68). The ruler of the empire was a deputy in a world order and had much in common with the 'powers' to which he scarcely seemed inferior (cf. *CH* XIII).

[3] VIII 63. Origen 'corrects' this from the Christian viewpoint (cf. VIII 31).

[4] VIII 35, 63, 65. Cf. Waser, p. 2011 (18 ff.) on the *daimones* as guardians of countries and cities.

[5] VIII 2, 13 f.; cf. Justin, *I Apol.* 5; Reicke, *Diakonie*, pp. 352 ff., esp. 358.

[6] Cf. Waser, p. 2012 (31 ff.); Reicke, *Diakonie*, p. 356; *Disobedient Spirits*, pp. 85 ff., 131.

[7] VIII 32. Cf. Athenagoras, *Apol.* 24. In *Celsus* VIII 34 it is observed that the Greeks say every man is born under a *daimon* (cf. *CH* XVI 15; XII 6; Nock-F, p. 185 n. 13). Origen corrects the view by citing Matt. 18.10 and Ps. 34.8; they are rather under *angels*.

he has represented a much more logical system than the prevailing secular one, for he is free from the ethical confusion of the same *daimones* working both good and evil in their ordained responsibilities; Origen's angels are good and his *daimones* are evil. This ethical distinction was not his first interest but was basic to his defence of Christianity over against a paganism which founded its claim upon the cosmic order. While Judaism looked upon the gods of the nations as the appointed spiritual rulers (folk angels), Paul appears to have preferred a tradition which dissociated Christianity from this more congenial view of paganism (Deut. 32.17; Ps. 106.37; I Cor. 10.20), yet his distinction was by no means so highly developed or systematically applied as was Origen's. 'It is not according to the law of God that any demon has had a share in worldly affairs, but it was by their own lawlessness that they perhaps sought out for themselves places. . . .'[1] Yet in this unofficial capacity the *daimones* are not without a positive usefulness in the rule of God: 'demons . . . in the capacity of public executioners receive power at certain times to carry out divine judgments.'[2]

With regard to civil rulers Origen does not set forth a complete system in refutation of Celsus,[3] but we can observe that the universe is under the guardianship of certain 'invisible agents' and, in his tendency to substitute angels for demons, he proceeds to identify 'the true rulers and generals and ministers' as 'angels of God' (VIII 31 f., 36). While Celsus earlier identified these officials as rulers 'in the air and upon earth' (VIII 35), Origen avoids making his view of divine government through angels parallel to the familiar *daimon* conception in every detail. It is of particular significance that he mentions the contemporary view that 'what is called the fortune of the king is a *daimon*',[4] and explains that it is basically because *daimones* are what pagans call 'gods' that Christians cannot swear by the 'fortune' of the emperor. It is this issue which appears to underlie the necessity of Origen's distinction. On the one hand he knows no other cosmological system than the

[1] *Celsus* VIII 33. Cf. *CH* IX 3, 5; contrast XVI 15.
[2] *Celsus* VIII 31. Cf. *CH* cited on p. 83 n. 3 above. Philo discusses tyrants in the same terms (see below).
[3] *Celsus* VIII 65; it is not immediately to the point to do so.
[4] VIII 65. Cf. VIII 6; Tarn, *Hel. Civ.*, p. 280; Nock, 'Divine *Comes*', pp. 112 f.; Pearson, 'Demons and Spirits', *op. cit.*, p. 592.

prevailing one, but on the other he must account for the fact that within that world order Christians do not subscribe to its 'logical' implications, e.g. honouring the emperor through the established cult. It was thus the early Christian acceptance of the prevailing cosmology but not pagan religion which demanded a rethinking of the place of *daimones* in the Cosmos. By replacing them in the world order with angels the cosmology was not altered, ethical confusion was eliminated, and paganism was shown to be unauthorized.[1] While Origen is firm in the view that rulers are appointed by God,[2] the problem of whether the king is under the guardianship of angels (because of his divine appointment) or under the authority of *daimones* (because of the evidence of tyranny [*Celsus* VIII 65] as well as his place in pagan religion) may account for his not entering at this point into what would necessarily be a detailed argument.[3] Justin (*I Apol.* 14) considers domination by *daimones* to be the actual situation in which the rulers find themselves (*I Apol.* 5.1; cf. 14.1; 44.12; 63.10; *II Apol.* 12.3; *Dial.* 18.3; 78.9), but his exhortation that the rulers free themselves from captivity by the *daimones* implies that personal subjection to them is not, from the Christian viewpoint, incumbent on the office-holder.[4] However, the general displacement of *daimones* by other spiritual guardians leaves open the question of what the 'ideal' relationship between the ruler and the divine order would be, if such was ever formulated.

The significance of these views, which are relatively late for our purposes, lies not in the contemporary value of their argument, but in the character of the world and State agreed upon by both pagans and Christians. Their differences were almost exclusively theological; the Christian gospel has never been based on a particular cosmology, but was proclaimed as intelligible to the accepted views of its own age.[5] The similarity of Origen's position

---

[1] *Celsus* VIII 13; cf. Athenagoras, *Apol.* 25, Justin, *I Apol.* 5.
[2] *Celsus* VIII 68, on the basis of Dan. 2.21, Ecclus. 10.4.
[3] Origen evidently accepts the fact that Antoninus Pius was divinely appointed as ruler, but he presses Celsus for the proof that worship of this emperor as a god was divinely appointed; VIII 9.
[4] Cf. 'Titles and *Proskynesis*' in Appendix A. The titles which relate civil authorities to the cosmic power structure are *ex officio*, not personal. The problem of the Christian as magistrate is not Paul's, however, and belongs chiefly to a later period.
[5] Sasse, p. 887 (3–34).

against Celsus to the earlier Jewish definitions of their faith in a pagan world—as well as the prevailing interest in theology rather than cosmology—is important as we observe not only the same primacy of theological interest in Paul, but essentially the same fundamental Graeco-Roman conception of the world ruler.

A. D. Nock contributes to our understanding from his valuable study of 'The Emperor's Divine *Comes*'. He first observes an *official*, but for us rather late, designation of 'this or that deity as *comes* Augusti' on coins and inscriptions.¹ *Comes*, 'when used of a deity in relation to the emperor, denotes a relationship, and one vouchsafed by the deity, who could go with the emperor on his ways and who could guard him on the march or on the seat of authority.'² The *comes* concept is particularly appropriate in its relationship to the emperor at a time when the supreme god was believed to govern through subordinates.³

(His *numen* and *maiestas*) were what they were because of the parallel higher permanent *numen* and *maiestas* above and behind them, because God's hand upheld God's Vicar. . . . The emperor, however exalted, was *minor*; he was born; he came to the throne through the *providentia* of the gods or through the correlative lower *providentia* of his predecessor.⁴

This material evidence clearly shows acceptance of the idea that the emperor was under a *conservator*, '*Schutzherr*'.⁵

On the basis of this late *official* view we have reason to expect that the conception of the emperor's domination by a spiritual superior enjoyed earlier a considerable period of unofficial popularity.⁶ Cicero showed from the fact that the gods cared for all

¹Nock, 'Divine *Comes*', p. 102.
²*Ibid.*, p. 103. On a possible background, cf. Frankfort, *Kingship*, pp. 303 f. and n. 35.
³Nock, 'Divine *Comes*', p. 104; cf. n. 21: Coins (late second century) show Hercules' hand on the shoulder of Commodus as his divine protector (*BMC* IV, p. 746. The two figures also appear in Janiform type: Genechi II.66 no. 131). In 191 (*BMC* IV, p. clxix) Jupiter is cited as *sponsor securitatis Augusti, defensor salutis Augusti*. Stauffer makes a remarkable use of coins to show the cosmic context of the common longing for salvation and how it was turned to political propaganda for Augustus (pp. 86–89)! Caesar's putting his own image on a coin was in itself a bold step (p. 126); cf. Antony's coin (showing the head of Antony together with that of the Sun god): 'Such a coin is both a confession and a programme' (p. 64).
⁴Nock, 'Divine *Comes*', p. 105.
⁵*Ibid.*, p. 105.
⁶Cf. Goodenough, 'Hellenistic Kingship', p. 98 n. 136.

men everywhere that they likewise were concerned for them in their divisions, sub-groups, and as individuals.¹ For this reason epic heroes had 'certain gods as companions (*comites*) in their perils and adventures'.² Apollonius said that he considered Athene to be the emperor's guardian,³ and Nock considers her prominence on Domitian's coins to be comparable to that of Hercules on coins of Commodus, although the word *comes* is wanting from the former.⁴ While there are numerous examples of divine presence with commoners,⁵ this relationship in the Graeco-Roman period was especially appropriate to the rulers.⁶ Horace (*Epp.* II 2. 187 ff.) is concerned with this same idea in terms of *genius*, which 'acquired more of the range of meaning possessed by *daimon*'.⁷

Again it is the idea of the *daimon* which seems basic to the Graeco-Roman conception of the emperor in his role of world ruler.⁸ But as with other terms from this period we cannot force upon it modern categories. The word appears at one time as an expression of the self, but at other times as a spiritual power which is beside the person.

Various as were the meanings of daimon, *it was a single word with a fluidity of usage and capacity of bearing at one and the same time senses which we distinguish and of passing imperceptibly from one to another.*⁹

¹*De Natura Deorum* II 164 ff.
²*Ibid.*, II 166.
³Philostratus, *Life of Apollonius* VII 32.
⁴'Divine *Comes*', p. 106. Cf. the Cancelleria relief, *American Journal of Archaeology* 44, 1940, fig. 2, p. 378.
⁵Nock, 'Divine *Comes*', p. 107, cites *Od.* XIX 398, IX 270 f., VII 165, 181; Plato, *Soph.* 216 A–B; Aristides, *To Zeus* 26, etc. Cf. Poimandres' presence with Hermes everywhere (*CH* I 3).
⁶Nock, 'Divine *Comes*', p. 107. As a man's genius left him at death so did Dionysus leave Antony (Plutarch, *Ant.* 75) and Minerva leave Domitian (Suetonius, *Domit.* 15.3). Nock adds a short bibliography in notes 50 f.
⁷Nock, 'Divine *Comes*', p. 109. Cf. also Rose, '*Numen*', p. 249; Tarn, 'Ruler-Cult and the Daemon', pp. 206–19.
⁸The interest in Plato, which revived in the second and first centuries BC, is credited by Nock ('Divine *Comes*', pp. 110 f.) with bringing to light again the concept of *daimones* which was to achieve such significance in the Graeco-Roman period. (On acceptance of this by Philo, cf. Bréhier, p. 22). Besides the word's appropriateness to the leading conceptions of the time, as illustrated above, Nock observes that its likeness to *genius*, which had already a firm place in formal religious language of Rome, accounts for its popularity and broad influence. Cf. Nock, 'Roman Army', pp. 240 f.
⁹Nock, 'Divine *Comes*', p. 110 (italics mine). 'A man's *daimon* could be a god. It is not, indeed, said that such a *daimon* could be identified with a

The Powers That Be

It is in the Graeco-Roman conception of the *daimon* (*genius*, *comes*) that we see the significance of all the preceding discussion in this chapter. The wide acceptance of this belief as a basic fact of the cosmic order is evident, not only from the variety of literature in which it appears, but from the matter-of-fact character of its use. This is especially important with regard to the early Christian and Jewish writers who, though they, like the philosophers, were forced to refine certain aspects to assure ethical and religious consistency, never doubted the basic correctness of the existence of the *daimones* or their place in the world order. While Christians and Jews found it necessary to differentiate the 'good *daimones*' as angels, it is of real significance that the *daimon* behind the emperor was so basic to the nature of the world and the State as they saw it, that the term was not replaced by another. Of all the applications of the concept of *daimones* or *comites*, none was more prominent or more widely accepted than that which had to do with the *daimon* of the emperor. While Christians could insist that it was the God and Father of our Lord Jesus Christ who appointed the emperor, they did not deny that the emperor was under the guardianship of a *daimon*, and this belief had no small significance for the Christian problem of 'honouring the emperor' without being involved in a religious recognition. Doubtless the most important factor in differentiating between angels and *daimones* was the reality of the latter. A. D. Nock has shown clearly that the idea of the *daimon* was basic to the Graeco-Roman conception of the emperor, but especially that this term was used with a 'fluidity' which is foreign to the modern mind yet thoroughly in keeping with the Graeco-Roman period. This is of utmost importance for any who desire to enter into the communication between Paul and the Romans with regard to the State.

The divinity of the emperor.—This much has been written concerning the idea of the place of the State in the Cosmos without mention of 'deification' of the emperor or the emperor-cult, for we believe that this conception of the ruler should not overshadow the important developments which we have just

---

specific deity. . . . Nevertheless a man's *daimon* was of the same kind as a namable divine companion, and *daimon* was a word for either' (*ibid.*, p. 111). Cf. Nock, 'Ruler-Cult', p. 35.

mentioned, but rather be understood within their context.¹

The extended controversy between classicists and orientalists as to the origin of this phenomenon is partly due to a difference as to what is meant by deification. To McEwan, who defends the orientalists' position, deification is primarily associated with the ruler-cult, and consequently is extremely old. To Ferguson, who supports the classicists, deification is actually the elevation of a ruler to the position of a god, especially the personal identification of the ruler with a particular god. Therefore, with a few exceptions, this development reached its climax relatively late and, in Rome especially, was long considered an extreme and fanatical claim on the part of a ruler. With the exception of Egypt, where the pharaoh was always a god, Alexander was first proclaimed a god in Greece, and this *during his lifetime*. At the same time, in the East he adopted the Persian royal position as the vicegerent of the gods, to be elevated to 'divinity' only after his death. In both instances Alexander was making the most of established tradition, not merely for self-glorification, but primarily for political reasons. The political value of receiving divine honours and promoting a ruler-cult throughout the realm was appreciated in the period of the empire as well, and continued to be the dominant purpose of what is loosely called 'deification'.² By elevating the monarch to a position above the ordinary populace, autonomous communities, it was hoped, would retain a sense of liberty; rule by a 'god' was of a completely different order from rule by a tyrant. To peoples who had been under the rule of a dynasty, however, the association of the ruler with the gods indicated his legitimate succession as a divine choice, and the office was removed from the grasp of the politically ambitious. This orientation of the cult to such practical service meant it was altered with the political needs of the time and the people.³ 'Political thought obliterated more and more

---

[1]See the appendix (A) for a summary of certain details on this large question.

[2]Cf. Nock, 'Ruler-Cult', p. 22. Glover (p. 153) cites Cicero (*Nat. Deorum* I 42, 118): '[it has been held that] the whole belief in immortal gods was invented by wise persons in the interest of the state,' and Varro (*ap.* Aug. *Civ. Dei* IV 27, VI 5): 'it is for the good of states that men should be deceived in religion.' Cf. Cochrane, pp. 101 f., and the position of the Sophists in Kleinknecht and Gutbrod, 'νόμος', *TWNT* IV, 1022 (14 ff.).

[3]Ferguson, pp. 15, 22; Charlesworth, pp. 14 f., 18; Tarn, *Hel. Civ.*, p. 279; Goodenough, *Politics of Philo*, pp. 44–46.

completely the distinction between what was human and what was divine.'¹ But nowhere was the confusion more likely than on that level where a human wielded unprecedented power under divine appointment.

In the period with which we are concerned, the 'deification' of the emperor is chiefly the official public activity we associate with the ruler-cult. In the light of its basically political purpose, we should evaluate the extravagant use of titles, including that of 'god', and such demonstrations of loyalty as *proskynesis*.

For our purposes, then, it is highly significant that the ruler-cult and other forms of honouring the emperor were not conceived by the hierarchy of a political bureaucracy and forced upon the minds of the masses, but rather the official circles of the Roman government were slow, cautious, even reluctant to engage in these practices, permitting them only for the practical political advantage which they yielded. For this means that the basic support for the political cult lay deeply embedded in the *Weltanschauung* of the people, especially in the widely accepted conception of world order. The problem of the Roman government was not so much how to hoodwink the masses as how to control their enthusiasm. If literary men are reserved in their acclaim of the emperor's divinity or of his place in the divine order of the universe, it is more likely because of the popularity than the uniqueness of this potentially dangerous concept. However, for the irresponsible non-literary masses there was no problem; the place of the emperor in the order of the universe was implicit in their view of the world in which they lived.² Wherever they travelled, the imperial symbols reminded them that local justice and order was by the grace of the emperor. The very coins which supported vast commercial intercourse and guaranteed food for the bearer were engraved with his name and image. To be subject to the emperor was not a matter of choice, but a dispensation of providence. In establishing an official cult, the Roman government yielded to a broad unquestioned conception of world order in which the

¹Ferguson, p. 16; cf. McEwan, p. 25.

²'What is called *Kaisermystik* implies that it was thought and hoped that the divine acted on a large scale through the power of Rome and its concrete manifestation in individual emperors . . . Rome and the emperor stood to the *numen deorum* as the Christian church stood to God and Christ' (Nock, 'Roman Army', p. 239).

To the Romans

supreme ruler of the Empire was associated with other 'world rulers' as a 'minister of God'.

In its various forms, the Graeco-Roman concept of the world was developed with the aid of a popularized form of science, a widespread philosophical system, and a variety of superstitions, with the only demand for consistency arising from human experience. It was in fact the realization that ancient modes of thought no longer comprehended the actual world of the Hellenistic period which stimulated the vast readjustment reflected in the discussion above. And the basic factor then, as in more ancient times, was the civil order. As has been demonstrated, the breaking down of national barriers made inadequate the nationalistic religions and cosmologies; the concept of empire promoted the trend to monotheism. The actual character of the world called forth the best thought of the Stoics as well as the ingenuity of astrologers, but in the resulting world view of universal dimensions the world state was the largest and most dominant factor.

The clear conclusion of the immediate study is that on the common level, where learned political theories were not formulated, the emperor shared in the ordering of a living universe by divine appointment. His authority was not merely the highest among men, but specifically established by God for the benefit of men. Civil obedience in the Graeco-Roman period meant subjection to the appointed powers among whom the emperor ranked as a ruler of men and a subordinate to gods. This subjection was participation in a divine order, a means to harmony with God and to salvation.[1]

Hellenistic Judaism.—Our concern with the concept of the State in the Cosmos in the Graeco-Roman world would not be complete, especially as we are concerned with Paul and the early Church, without mention of Hellenistic Judaism.[2]

The *vocabulary* of Hellenistic Judaism as reflected in the Septuagint illustrates remarkably the adaptation of Jewish faith to the new world of the Hellenistic period. With regard to the discussion above (and in ch. I) we should observe the LXX translation of the phrase *Yahweh*

---
[1] Charlesworth, p. 42. Cf. Plutarch above, p. 79.
[2] We cannot even begin to consider the question of the degree of Diaspora Hellenization, or even the more immediate matter of the Jews in Rome (cf. the bibliog. in appendix B and the works by Dodd and Goodenough in the bibliography to this chapter). In this section only 'sample' notes are made.

Sabaoth. Particularly important is the rendering of *Sabaoth* as 'powers' (I–IV Kgd., Pss., Amos, Zech., Jer.). Dodd comments, 'We recognize here the monotheistic tendency to represent the gods of polytheism as aspects or agencies of the one supreme Being.'[1] The translators appear to have understood this word to indicate divine agencies. Dodd continues:

> It is surely as such that they appear in lists of the angelic orders, along with ἀρχαί, ἐξουσίαι, κυριότητες. Thus we recognize a tendency in Judaism, parallel with the monotheistic tendency which we have noted in paganism, to represent subordinate supernatural beings (the 'gods' of paganism, the 'angels' of Judaism) as 'powers' or 'agencies' of the one God, and in this sense δυνάμεις. ... We may fairly suspect that the translators were willing to meet half-way a growing usage in paganism, by which the gods were reduced to powers or agencies of the one god, and that in the expression κύριος τῶν δυνάμεων they intended to suggest an idea similar to that expressed in the phrases κύριος κυρίων, θεὸς θεῶν.[2]

The term 'powers' appears particularly interesting because of its ambiguities. Dodd feels that its choice for the translation of *Yahweh Sabaoth* may have been precisely because of this, for 'as a matter of fact there is evidence that *there was in Hellenistic Judaism a tendency to oscillate between the abstract and the concrete in conceiving these heavenly beings*'.[3] Another but less frequent translation of *Sabaoth* is παντοκράτωρ,[4] which 'means the One who controls or rules all things, perhaps with κοσμοκράτωρ in mind: the one God rules and controls all other cosmic powers'.[5]

A similar observation may be made concerning the use of 'angels' in the LXX as a convenient translation of *elohim* where it appeared in an objectionable context or where its plurality was awkward (Pss. 137 (EVV 138). 1; 96 (EVV 97). 7; 8.6). Significantly it was also used to translate the idiom *bene elohim*,[6] confirming its association with the term 'powers'.[7] Some light is cast upon Hellenistic Judaism by the use of '*cosmos*' in Wisdom. It is a term comprehending the elements of nature,

---

[1] Dodd, p. 17; cf. Grundmann, pp. 293 (37)–294 (9); Waser, p. 2012 (10 ff.).
[2] Dodd, p. 18 f., Pss. 102 (EVV. 103). 21, 148. 2–3. Cf. Grundmann, pp. 297 (4–21), 298 (21–38).
[3] Dodd, p. 110 (italics mine); cf. Reicke, *Diakonie*, p. 357.
[4] II, III Kingdoms, I Chron., minor prophets, Jer. Cf. Michaelis, 'κοσμοκράτωρ', and 'παντοκράτωρ', *TWNT* III, 913 f.
[5] Dodd, p. 19.
[6] Gen. 6.2; Deut. 32.8; Job 1.6, 2.1; Dan. 3.92 (25); Dodd, pp. 22 f., 223 f.
[7] Moulton-M, 'ἄγγελος'; Dodd, pp. 21–23.

which the pagans considered to be 'the gods that rule the world' (Wisd. 13.2; 16.17). Wisdom did not set aside the contemporary belief, but, following the precedent of the Old Testament, it adapted the cosmology of the time to monotheistic Judaism. God, the Lord, ruled the Cosmos and caused it to fight on behalf of his people.[1] While there are other words which could be presented, these suffice to show how greatly Jews in the Graeco-Roman period shared in the contemporary views of the Cosmos. Jewish concepts of great antiquity were thus given an effective expression for world-wide Judaism.

Philo has never made a noteworthy impression as a politician.[2] Nevertheless, there is much to be learned from him concerning the politics of Hellenistic Judaism and its conception of the State in the Cosmos.[3] If Philo is not conspicuously concerned with civil government, it is not to be wondered at, for critical views were dangerous to hold and foolish to express.[4] Subjection to pagan lords is expedient for the moment,[5] but there is every indication beneath the flattery that the Jews of Alexandria would have the civil order other than it was.

Philo's conception of rulership clearly belongs to the same world with which we have been concerned. The one God[6] ruled through his powers,[7] and civil government was to be comprehended in these terms.[8] 'The cosmic imperium could be entrusted to an individual

---

[1] Wisd. 5.17, 20; 16.17, 24; 19.6; cf. Judg. 5.20. Wisd. 18.24 f. is explained in Philo, *Vita Mos.* II 117–26. The LXX in certain instances has translated *saba* as *cosmos*, making the deities which other countries honour as gods part of the cosmic order (cf. Deut. 4.19; 17.3; Isa. 24.21; 40.26; Gen. 2.1).

[2] Bréhier, p. 32. Contrast Bréhier (pp. 18–23) with Goodenough (*Politics of Philo*, p. 46 n. 11); cf. Schmidt, *Polis*, pp. 91–94 for a survey of views on Philo as a politician.

[3] Here we are indebted again to E. R. Goodenough for his study in this field, *Politics of Philo*, which forms part of an extensive work beginning with 'Hellenistic Kingship'.

[4] *Som.* II 83, 88 f.; Goodenough, *Politics of Philo*, p. 5.

[5] *Som.* II 89 f., 78 ff., 92. Cf. Goodenough, *Politics of Philo*, pp. 40 f. On Philo's agreement with the apocalyptic writers in this regard, cf. *ibid.*, pp. 25, 115 ff.

[6] Philo follows the Hellenistic monotheistic argument in proving the unity of God from the unity of the world. (*Conf.* 170).

[7] *Conf.* 171. While God does the great and good things himself, the secondary and especially the corrective and punitive are carried out through these ministers (angels) (*Conf.* 181 f., *Leg. Alleg.* III 177 f., *Fug.* 66; cf. Colson's note *a* (*Philo*, LCL IV, 110); Grundmann, 'ἄγγελος', *TWNT* I, 74 (12–24); above p. 83 n. 3.

[8] E.g. *Prov.* II 37–41 (cf. frag. ap. Eusebius, *Praep. Evang.* VIII 14.37–41). God appoints tyrants just as good governors appoint public executioners (cf. *Abr.* 143 f., *Legat.* 56). Philo integrates this with his doctrine of providence (*Flac.* 170, 191). Cf. Bréhier, pp. 19–23, 39.

The Powers That Be

nation for a term, as that nation dominated all men for a time.'[1] This is the familiar pattern which originated in Mesopotamia and spread through the Hellenistic world on the tide of astrology, monotheism, and the belief in powers. In Philo we have a particularly clear view of the Hellenistic conception of the ideal ruler. The king is a shepherd,[2] father of his people,[3] the ultimate owner of all property of the realm,[4] and, as in the case of Augustus, '*Soter* and *Euergetes*'.[5] It is noteworthy that these same titles are applied to God.[6] Philo observes:

In his material substance the king is just the same as any man, but in the authority of his rank he is like God of all.[7] For there is nothing upon earth more exalted than he. Since he is mortal, he must not vaunt himself; since he is a god, he must not give way to anger. For if he is honoured as being an image of God, yet he is at the same time fashioned from the dust of the earth, from which he should learn simplicity to all.[8]

---

[1] Goodenough, *Politics of Philo*, p. 77; cf. *Light*, pp. 38 f.; above pp. 17–20, 70 ff.

[2] *Jos.* 2 f. (cf. 38 f.); *Decal.* 40–43; *Spec.* IV 176 (170 ff.); *Agr.* 50; Ex. 22.22–24, etc. Cf. Dio Chrys., *Orat.* II 77 (cf. I. 15–20); Diotogenes ap. Stob. IV 7.62; 2.24; Goodenough, *Politics of Philo*, pp. 45, 95. Knox (p. 88 and its n. 1) relates this to the contemporary view of gods as 'kings' of various spheres of life.

[3] *Spec.* IV 184; frag. ap. Eusebius, *Praep. Evang.* VIII 14.2, 3; cf. Sthenidas ap. Stob. IV 7.63; Dio Chrys., *Orat.* I 22.40; Diotogenes ap. Stob. IV 7.61 f.; Bréhier, p. 19.

[4] *Plant.* 54–57; *Spec.* IV 159. Cf. Diotogenes ap. Stob. IV 7.26; Ecphantus ibid., 64; Goodenough, *Politics of Philo*, p. 94; 'Hellenistic Kingship', pp. 70, 76.

[5] *Flac.* 74; cf. *Legat.* 140–61 (contrast 162 ff.); Bréhier, p. 22; Goodenough, *Politics of Philo*, pp. 14 f.; Knox, p. 37 and its n. 3. These titles were given *ex officio* to Flaccus (*Flac.* 126) and Gaius (*Legat.* 19–22).

[6] *Opif.* 169; *Leg. Alleg.* II 56; *Decal.* 41; etc. The 'saving' rule of God (*Conf.* 98; *Abr.* 70; *Jos.* 149; *Decal.* 60, 155; *Praem.* 34 where universal providence is compared to a well ordered state) is a model for the order of government (*Decal.* 14; *Jos.* 149). See above the contemporary view that the king was to imitate God and correspond to him upon earth. Cf. Bréhier, pp. 19 f.

[7] This dual nature of the ruler is reflected elsewhere, the human aspect dominating the actual situation, the divine aspect the ideal. Contrast the Joseph of *Som.* II (e.g. 78 ff.) with the Joseph of *Jos.* (e.g. 2 f.). Cf. Colson, *Philo*, LCL VI, xiii, on this 'chronic tendency to see both sides of a question alternately or even simultaneously'. On 'oscillation' between the abstract and concrete as characteristic of Hellenistic Judaism and Philo, cf. Dodd, pp. 18, 110 f.; Grundmann, 'δύναμις', C, 2 (pp. 299 f.); cf. Nock and Nilsson above, pp. 81 f., 88 f.

[8] A frag. of Philo preserved by Antony, *Melissa*, Ser. CIV, text and translation in Goodenough, *Politics of Philo*, p. 99. Goodenough makes extensive comparisons with the Pythagoreans in his ch. V (e.g. Ecphantus ap. Stob. IV 6.22); see also his pp. 58, 62, 94; *Light*, pp. 38 f.; Bréhier, p. 19.

To the Romans

This evidence of Philo's political thought does not appear strange, whether it is compared with contemporary pagan belief or with the faith and life of Judaism in the Graeco-Roman period. What we have seen of Philo's views on the State leads us to believe that he as well as his contemporaries of less learning accepted to a high degree the Graeco-Roman view of the State in the Cosmos wherever it did not oppose the essential faith of Judaism. This is made even more impressive by the fact that the offensive aspects of the pagan view of the State were not so much rejected, leaving a serious gap in the contemporary *Weltanschauung*, as reinterpreted in a way acceptable to the Jewish faith. Had 'patchwork' not been done in this manner, Judaism, and possibly Christianity, would have been forced to construct a whole new cosmology. This was not necessary, however, for both religions received the contemporary cosmic system and the political view compounded with it, making such amendments and interpretations as were necessary.

Among the *archeological* data of specific relevance to the State we observe only that in Rome[1] as in Egypt[2] it was thought proper (and advantageous) to dedicate synagogues in honour of rulers and other persons of authority. The history of Jewish expulsions from Rome is evidence that the Jews did not consider the rule of Rome to be the ultimate end of Providence, but on the other hand, as shown above and in ch. I, they could share in the contemporary view that the ruler was appointed by God. The history of special privilege granted the Jews by the emperors would serve to confirm this in their thought.

In those elements of Hellenistic Judaism we have set forth we have been struck by the universality and the authority of the Graeco-Roman world-view. The sciences had been liberated from the particular religious views of separate peoples and had acquired an independent authenticity which no major religion of the period, including the Jews, could ignore. While the Jews refused to share in the religious syncretism of the period, they appear to have shared fully in the Graeco-Roman conception of the Cosmos,

[1] Among the twelve or thirteen congregations known to have existed in Rome about the first century AD are the Augustesians, Volumnians, Agrippesians, Severians (?Herodians).

[2] There are three early examples: Alexandria (37 BC), Athribis (second century BC), and Shedia (247–222 BC). These are discussed by Goodenough, *Jewish Symbols*, II 84–88. At Athribis an additional plaque was found reading, 'In honour of King Ptolemy and of Queen Cleopatra and their children, Hermias and his wife Philotera and their children (have consecrated) this bench (*exedra*) and the synagogue.' Cf. Philo, *Legat.* 133 f. (138); *Flac.* 48 f. (41 f.).

expressing in terms as nearly their own as possible the widespread belief in power, cosmic order, and the rule of one God. Although the Jews did not share in the emperor-cult, the evidence we have presented above shows that they could agree with their neighbours that rulers were divinely appointed, and that the State had its assigned place in a providential cosmic order; the Jews could honour their rulers within the context of their faith. While these views were radically affected by their reorientation in the Jewish and the Christian beliefs, they were however received, not as peculiarly Jewish or Christian, but as views held by men everywhere.

At the beginning of chapter III we observed that the results of sound scholarship in the field of late Judaism and the New Testament had been accepted by both sides of the controversy over Romans 13. Inasmuch as the substance of this chapter represents nothing essentially new or radical in the way of Hellenistic studies we have every reason to expect that it will prove acceptable to all concerned, and thus constitute the basis for an exegetical solution.

Our survey of the concept of the State in the Graeco-Roman world has positive significance for our interpretation of Romans 13. If we are to be a party to Paul's communication with the church in Rome we must enter into a world in which we cannot make radical distinctions between myth and history, material and spiritual, as we do today. It was a well known fact in antiquity that the same word was used, not only to indicate 'both' spiritual and material elements, but to symbolize the inseparable relationship between the spiritual and material worlds. The unity of the Cosmos, a concept drawn from the political unity of the world, not only encouraged a religious monotheism but emphasized the place of the State and its ruler in the universal order. It was only natural in this context to look upon rulers as 'ministers of God for the care and safety of mankind'. Men, no less than things, were under the influence of spiritual rulers (*daimones*) and nowhere was this more applicable or significant than in relation to the emperor. Again with regard to the ruler we observe the fluidity of the terminology characteristic of the period. The same work could be attributed at one time to the king, at another to his *daimon*; it was through the divine power behind the emperor that he received his character and his power. We are impressed by the degree to which Jews (and Christians) shared in the Graeco-Roman world-view. In particular, the concept of the emperor as subordinate to a universe under the order of one God suited their monotheistic outlook well, and the Jews could dedicate their houses of worship to God in honour of the rulers he had established in the firm belief that he who appointed kings would also bring the greater day for which they longed.

It is our conviction, from the evidence given in this chapter, that there was a common Graeco-Roman concept of the State; its ruler was divinely appointed in relation to a cosmic system of spiritual powers. All the evidence so favours the wide acceptance of this world view that where Paul, Hellenistic Jews, or early Christians do not openly oppose it we should first of all assume that it was taken for granted until it is found incompatible in some particular. For no fundamental concept of this time seems more a part of the great main-stream of Hellenistic thought or more shaped by the popular acceptance of astrology, monotheism, and a dynamic world order, than the Graeco-Roman concept of the State in the Cosmos. Precisely because the form of the State was so basic to their understanding of the world in which they lived, men under the Roman empire could not abstract the State from the universe as they saw it. To think of the emperor in another fashion, e.g., as we look upon governing authorities today, would be no small abstraction; it would be to pull the foundations out from under the Graeco-Roman *Weltanschauung*. If we are to appreciate the world in which the Church was born and spent its early years, it is imperative that we conceive of it as a Church in the Roman Empire. The corollary, so important for this study, is simply that *there can be no proper understanding of what early Christians, Jews, and their pagan contemporaries understood as the State, in particular as the* exousiai, *apart from that world view enveloping aeons and* daimones, *providence and powers, in which the ruler was both divine by appointment and human by birth, and the boundaries between the spirit world and the world of humanity and nature were fluid and often imperceptible.* This much is the clear result of our concern with the Graeco-Roman concept of the State in the Cosmos, and it is the unavoidable responsibility of exegesis to consider this result if we are to enter into Paul's communication.

THE WRITER AND THE READERS OF THE EPISTLE

Our emphasis upon the exegesis of Romans 13.1–7 from the standpoint of the problem of communication makes the consideration of the writer and readers of the epistle imperative. However, our study of the Graeco-Roman concept of the State in the Cosmos has made the traditional 'introductory' questions of author, occasion, and destination less crucial than would ordinarily be the case. For example, the Jewish or Gentile character of the Roman church is not a decisive question when it is seen that the cosmology of Jews and pagans was basically the same, and that for both groups the State played a significant part, by divine appointment, in the established order of things. Plutarch, Philo, Paul, and Jewish apocalyptic could refer to rulers as 'ministers of God', and Christians gave ample support to this view in their early writings as they drew upon an old biblical tradition of God's work through rulers of all kinds. Christians differed from pagans in their views of the State, as did the Jews before them; likewise their view of the Cosmos was distinctive; but the peculiarities of the Christian outlook were consequences of their conviction that Jesus is Lord. Without denying the radical character of this confession, we find in the form in which it was conceived a firm reaffirmation of the prevailing world view: Jesus' lordship was understood in terms of the principalities and powers. The Jewish conception of folk angels is hardly different; it is nothing more than a formulation of the Jewish hope in terms which were common in the Graeco-Roman world. There are a number of questions for which the composition and character of the Roman church, whether Jewish or Gentile in background, will remain important, but ours is not one of them; we need only to know that this is a Christian letter written to Rome about the middle of the first century. That the Christian interpretation of the 'facts' was quite different from that of the surrounding world should not be confused with the practically universal contemporary agreement as to what those facts were. The unity of the Graeco-Roman world assured Paul that he could write regarding the State with the same confidence that he would be understood as when he decided to write in the Greek language.

It now becomes clear that the well-worn problem of the domi-

To the Romans

nant characteristic in Paul's background is not especially significant for our passage, for the 'background' of our problem was common to pagan, Jew, and Christian. Once we take seriously the Graeco-Roman conception of the State in the Cosmos, the important thing is not Paul's background, but his 'foreground', not his Jewish or Hellenistic characteristics, but his Christian faith.

V

THE POWERS THAT BE

THE POINT OF DEPARTURE AND THE CONCLUDING PROBLEM

Our review of contemporary discussion of Romans 13.1-7 has revealed not only sharp disagreement, but a wide variety of approaches to the passage. These have ranged from the inoffensive objectivity of the history of religions to the more heated debate over the validity of thoroughly Christologically-founded theology. The political history of modern Europe has made a theological understanding of the State of urgent importance, and since the war a number of essays have struggled with the question.[1] The present essay, however, attempts to be nothing but exegetical and cannot undertake a proper consideration of all the problems into which the interpretation of our passage has been drawn.

As we discovered above,[2] the exegetical task regarding Romans 13.1-7 calls for its interpretation not only from the tradition of what Paul was *imparting* to Rome but from the broader context of the *communication*. Only in this way can what is imparted carry its intended meaning and our understanding be considered valid. To this end, the preceding chapter undertook to set forth a pertinent aspect of the Graeco-Roman understanding of the State and to determine to what extent Paul and the Roman church shared in it. By concentrating upon only one aspect of our problem, we attempted to dissolve the stalemate over the meaning of '*exousiai*'.

It is now evident that the political significance of the word, even for Paul and the Roman church, is implicated in the cosmic dimension of the Graeco-Roman concept of the State. *Exousiai* were powers, human and spiritual, divinely appointed to particular

---

[1] We have mentioned the positions of Wendland, Künneth, Perles; cf. above, p. 57, n. 3.
[2] Ch. III (e.g. pp. 56 f.) and pp. 63-68.

responsibilities in the cosmic order. Spiritual authorities were generally considered to lie behind the human ones, and the 'fluidity' of the terminology only emphasized the inseparable relationship between the spiritual and material in the one Cosmos. Subjection to the *exousiai* was therefore subjection to an established cosmic order, most clearly evident and commonly experienced in the rule of Rome.

In illustrating the necessity of dealing with our passage as a communication, we touched upon the other principal aspect of our problem: Paul expected the church at Rome to understand '*exousiai*' because they were citizens of the Graeco-Roman world; they would understand the word 'God' because they were Christians. It is the task of understanding this word 'God' in Romans 13.1–7 which will dominate our conclusion of this essay.

The importance of this aspect of our problem is rarely recognized except as it is related to the 'Christological foundation of the State', i.e. the question whether 'God' in our passage is to be interpreted as 'Christ'.[1] But the basic problem is inherent in the rather common 'exegetical' remark that Paul is really saying nothing new in our passage apart from the 'vigour' and earnestness of his words; the same admonition could have been written by a contemporary rabbi.[2]

It is the widespread acceptance of Romans 13.1–7 as in no way distinctively Christian which must now be put in question. For if the Graeco-Roman view of the State is a significant factor for understanding our passage, then can the early Christian faith in Christ's victory and lordship over the spiritual powers be any less decisive for understanding what Paul wrote to Rome concerning the State? The *cosmic* scope of the work of Christ in early Christian thought and the *cosmic* context of the State in contemporary thought forbid us any longer to ignore the significance of the Christian faith for a proper interpretation of the communication in Romans 13.1–7.

At this point it would be well to set forth the content of our passage in the light of our discussion thus far and the question in hand.

[1] Cf. pp. 51–54 above.
[2] E.g. von Campenhausen (cf. pp. 50 f. above) and Gaugler (II, 290) cf. p. 104 n. 5 below.

The Powers That Be

ROMANS 13.1-7

Introductory questions.—(1) This passage, though lacking specific syntactical connexion with what precedes,[1] nevertheless continues the exhortation[2] of the previous chapter, which is not so narrow and specific as to make the subject of 13.1-7 conspicuously irrelevant or abrupt. The larger context of the passage may be considered 'eschatological', concerned with the Christian life in the period before the consummation of Christ's lordship and the establishment of God's kingdom.[3] Christians should neither lose hope nor display fanatical disregard for the present order in anticipating the next.

(2) Any special reason for Paul's directing this exhortation to Rome is not immediately apparent (Knox, Gaugler), but there are several factors which give his words here particular relevance. (*a*) The name Rome itself suggests the subject of civil order.[4] (*b*) Not only was the gospel greatly valued in terms of Christian freedom, and in the light of the eschatological hope, subject to over-enthusiastic interpretation, but there may be evidence of a particular pride in independence at Rome.[5] (*c*) 'Foreign' groups and

---

[1]Meyer, Zahn, Godet (none is necessary), Denney, Parry, Gaugler, Michel. Some efforts are made at association, however: (*a*) Paul moves from considering duties common to the life of the Christian community to consider the duties of the individual (B. Weiss). (*b*) The subject is brought on by the idea that private vengeance is prohibited (Rom. 12.19; Garvie, Moule, Lagrange; cf. pp. 63-65 above). (*c*) Following the consideration of the Christian's restraint over against evil, Paul speaks of the State (O. Holtzmann, Zahn).

[2]Zahn and Althaus represent the view that Rom. 13.1-7 sets forth a 'general principle' and therefore has no connexion with the previous exhortation, esp. the theme of not conforming to this world (Michel, although he holds that Paul continues the eschatological theme of 12.1 f.).

[3]Cf. above, pp. 34 f., 48, 56.

[4]Cf. p. 12 n. 3; Parry.

[5]Jülicher, Zahn, Gaugler (see Rom. 12.3), Lietzmann, Althaus, Dodd. The influence of Jewish thought upon the early Christian mind is not clear in this regard. On the one hand, the Jews' love of freedom is well known, and many suggest that it influenced Christians (Knox, Meyer, Denney [cf. Deut. 17.15, Mark 12.14], Findlay, Parry, Lietzmann), quite apart from the question of the proportion of Jewish Christians in the Roman congregation (Garvie, however, represents the view that this paragraph is directed especially to Jewish converts). On the other hand it is widely recognized that Paul's words recommending obedience are in line with Jewish doctrine (Jülicher, Gaugler, von Campenhausen [see p. 103 n. 2 above]). While Dodd observes (citing Dan. 4.28, Wisd. 6.1-11, En. 4.65) that the Jews were more inclined to warn

religions could easily be suspected of disloyalty[1] and Paul was eager that no harm be done the cause of Christ in the empire by the carelessness of any one group of believers. His concern with the Christian's subjection to the State seems related to no particular crisis, but has all the naturalness of what appeared appropriate to the occasion of his writing.

(3) The direct simplicity of the paragraph forbids extreme interpretations.[2] (*a*) There is no clear limitation of Paul's words to the particular authorities who had jurisdiction over the particular Roman congregation at that particular time. (*b*) Likewise there is no evidence that Paul's words were wholly idealistic without any reference to prevailing circumstances. (*c*) There is no indication that Paul was speaking of the forms of government quite apart from its officers. (*d*) There is no reason to believe that Paul's view of the State would be lightly altered by troubled circumstances; he had suffered and Jesus had been put to death at the hand of the State, but Paul was peculiarly impressed by the hand of God in it all.[3] The absence of any qualification of his

---

governments of God's judgment than to recognize their divine appointment, it has been shown above (e.g. pp. 17 ff., 93 ff.) that the idea of divine ordinance was authentically (but not exclusively) Jewish.

Evidence in Romans may offer grounds for a view which cannot be developed in detail here. The *heilsgeschichtlich* theme of Rom. 9-11 is perhaps made necessary for the same reason that Paul is careful to identify Jesus as the Son of David, and himself as both a Jew by race and an apostle to the Gentiles by calling: namely, that the Roman community, which had a spontaneous origin, not only was independent of apostolic authority in particular, but was proud of its freedom from authority in general. Thus Paul must make clear that in his insistence upon the freedom of those who walk in the spirit (e.g, Rom. 8), he does not mean that the believer is without a vital relation to the history of redemption. Believers were not independent wild plants, but were engrafted into an older tradition of revelation and redemption, which eventually was again to include Israel. Likewise he had to make clear that, free as they were, they still were related to a larger secular community which was ordered by God, and they were expected to show their freedom by subjection to the ordinances of God for conscience' sake. This same spirit may also underlie their own designation (Kühl, Althaus) of certain brothers as weak on the grounds that they could not sever themselves from religious traditions. In this light, Romans 13 seems, on the one hand, very typical of Jewish policy; on the other hand, it is offered to a group which apparently is outside or revolting from the Jewish tradition in this as well as other respects.

[1] Acts 16.20 f.; 17.7; cf. p. 85 above.
[2] Cf. p. 39 n. 1.
[3] Knox, Findlay; cf. pp. 12 f. above.

words and his unfamiliarity with the local magistrates in Rome suggest that his words in our passage are of a general character (contrary to Michel). If men hold authority in the State, they are God's servants, for the State is part of the world order whose beginning and end and powers are divinely established.[1]

Paul's view of the State had deeper roots than our modern estimate of political parties. Our allegiance may be radically affected within the period of a few days if events alter our confidence, but for Paul the State belonged to an order within which the sun rose and set, and rain and wind, sickness and health were comprehended. Governments lost their authority and sanction when they were replaced by others, not when men suffered or attempted to make quick work of the problem of evil. The State as Paul knew it showed a variety of moods yet possessed more integrity than any other institution of his day. The eschatological character of Paul's thought excluded preoccupation with the concept of an 'ideal state'. So long as the world endured there would be a State, and there is no ground for believing Paul thought it would be any better or any worse, any more or less a servant of God, than it was when he wrote or had experienced it personally. For this reason the idea that Paul's paragraph presupposes 'normal conditions' (Denney) loses any real significance; the 'normal' conditions were the actual ones of 'this age' and therefore in no sense 'ideal'.[2] Paul's 'ideal' was the consummation of the Kingdom of God, and there was no place in that ideal for the work of Roman officials.[3] Paul continued his exhortation with regard to the Christian life (Rom. 12) to remind the Roman church that so long as it was proper to 'weep with those who weep', to be careful of one's behaviour in evil circumstances, to preach the gospel of Jesus Christ—so long as a Christian lived in 'this world' —he should be subject to the governing authorities.

What Paul was 'imparting'.—Paul's message may be paraphrased as follows.

---

[1] Althaus stresses correctly: *every* actual State in all its weakness. The paragraph is not a comprehensive ethic or political theory, but a pastoral word (cf. Kühl).

[2] Even the author of Revelation does not abandon the idea of 'demonic' rulers as servants of God, cf. Rev. 17.17.

[3] The 'ideal lion' was one which ate straw like an ox (cf. Isa. 65.25; p. 117 n. 2 below).

The Powers That Be

Everyone[1] ought to obey those who are superior[2] because of the authority of their office. For there is no one with a position of responsibility in the world order who has not been commissioned by God;[3] the whole structure of authority[4] in the world is God's work. Consequently, anyone who is insubordinate toward this authority is actually opposing what God himself has established, and persons guilty of such contempt will be the cause of their own[5] conviction and condemnation.[6] For it is not the intention of rulers to discourage what is good,[7] but to prevent what is bad. So if[8] you wish to be free from anxiety with regard to those who have power over you, then let your whole manner of living be marked by what is good, and instead of living in fear, you need expect only the goodwill of those who govern. The reason for this is precisely that an official is a servant whom God has appointed for

---

[1] Inclusiveness is emphasized (Kühl, Zahn, Gaugler). Christians, because they have life and breath and dwell within the limits of this age, are expected to contribute to its divinely established order by not opposing those who have been appointed to maintain it. The singular directs the exhortation to the individual (Sanday-H., Garvie, Kühl; 'every soul' is a Hebraism, cf. Acts 2.43; 3.23; Lev. 7.27; 17.12; Num. 6.6, 11).

[2] Not only the 'higher' authorities (Meyer, Weiss) but everyone in an official capacity with jurisdiction over us is to be respected and obeyed (Denney, Parry, Gaugler).

[3] Although the better MSS prefer ὑπό, a few commentators (Meyer, Godet) retain the Graeco-Latin reading of the TR (ἀπό). We read with א A B D C E L P al. vg. syr. cop. go. arm. aeth. Or. etc., Sanday-H. and most other modern commentators. On the matter of syntax, Denney (after Weiss) cites Bar. 4.27.

[4] 'Those which exist. . . .' The present participle does not stress limitation so much as relevance.

[5] Dative *incommodi* (Lagrange, Kühl, Lietzmann [citing *Mart. Polycarp* 4 and other passages]).

[6] While this obviously is to take place within the framework of the order which is violated (Meyer, Godet, Moule, Denney, Parry, Lagrange, Gaugler, Sanday-H.), the whole force of the paragraph insists that the civil judgment be seen as divinely authorized. Although 'opposing God' is sin, it is beyond the intention of this paragraph to evaluate civil disobedience in terms of 'eternal damnation'.

[7] Cf. Patrick Young's conjecture (based on the Ethiopic), favoured by Moffatt (trans.), Hort, (Dodd). The 'good' here is what the *rulers* recognize as good. The exhortation to do good, therefore, means not to violate this broad ethical standard by which the State fulfils its function. In the fulfilment of his Christian calling, the believer is to observe the nature of civil order and co-operate in its fulfilling its divine calling, the scope of which the Christian alone can fully appreciate.

[8] 'Do you wish. . . .' Probably a (rhetorical) question (Meyer [after Beza, Calvin. . . . Lachman, Tischendorf, Ewald, Hofmann], Sanday-H., Denney, Dodd). It is read as a statement by Kühl, Lietzmann (after Luther, Tholuck, Philippi, according to Meyer).

The Powers That Be

your[1] welfare. But if you should commit an offence, be prepared to live in fear, for it is no accident that he has the power to require your life.[2] But it is in this role as well that the public official is a servant of God, acting as an avenger and executing God's wrath[3] upon whoever does what is bad. Therefore,[4] you see how necessary it is for you to be obedient subjects. But do not obey merely from fear of the wrath, as if you were workers of evil or ignorant of these things, but obey for conscience' sake, as workers of what is good who know for what end authority exists. It is also for this reason[5] that it has been the custom[6] of Christians to pay what is officially required of them. For the governing officials are ministers[7] of God diligent in fulfilling the calling[8]

[1]Christians benefit from the State's function, although the State is not consciously concerned with benefiting Christians as such (Denney). This is made clear by Kühl and Zahn who associate σοί with εἰς τὸ ἀγαθόν rather than with διάκονος. The view of most commentators is made explicit by Dodd: the wrath exercised by the State is the principle of retribution inherent in a moral universe; but see below.

[2]'In vain. . . .' This does not refer to 'success' but to the power of the sword (not dagger) as particularly appointed by God (Kühl, Moule).

[3]Cf. the widespread opinion of the time concerning the instruments of divine vengeance (above, pp. 18 f., 86, 83 n. 3, 86 n. 2, 95 nn. 7 f.). While they serve God's purpose, they are characterized by their own wills, and are frequently evil *daimones*, who are held responsible for this activity. Therefore, that the State serves as God's servant for wrath in no way qualifies the character of the State itself, rather its calling and service are defined.

[4]διό, the logical result of the preceding: the officials are God's servants in world order.

[5]The reference of διὰ τοῦτο is sharply contested. While many (Meyer, Garvie, Moule, Sanday-H. [and Cornely and Kühl according to Lagrange]) maintain that the reference is to the immediately preceding statement, i.e., Christians pay their taxes for their conscience' sake, we prefer to read this phrase with Lietzmann (and Kühl?) in parallel with v. 5, i.e. (with Althaus, Zahn, Lagrange [and according to Meyer, Calvin, Tholuck, De Wette]) payment of taxes is not a result of conscientious subjection, but the evidence and practice of it, the ground for both being the same (cf. Lagrange: the second γάρ is causal, not the first). See nn. 4 and 8.

[6]The actual practice of Christians rests on the fact that civil government is part of God's order. However, τελεῖτε is read as an imperative by Zahn and Hofmann. It is not clear if Mark 12.17 or parallels (Dodd, Findlay, Garvie) were in mind or not. Cf. I Cor. 11.16, where actual practice is basic to Paul's explanation; but Lagrange maintains that Paul does not argue from fact to meaning here.

[7]While some (Garvie, Findlay, Meyer, Kühl, and Cornely [according to Lagrange]) feel that Paul intended to communicate the idea of the State's sacred (i.e. 'priestly') function, we prefer the identification of Lietzmann (followed by Parry, Denney, Zahn, Sanday-H., Gaugler), whose persuasive evidence indicates a public service (cf. also Liddell-S.). Lagrange objects that this identification is not wholly appropriate because such 'public service' was always without charge, whereas the State collects taxes. Therefore, he

The Powers That Be

we have described. Fulfil your obligations to everyone, paying tribute to whom it is required and taxes to the proper authorities.[1] Likewise know whom you should fear and whom you should honour, and fulfil your obligation.

Elements in Communication.—We have already discussed the fact that there are elements in communication which are necessary to a full understanding of what is imparted, but which nevertheless are not subject to 'indexing' nor likely to be carried in the tradition of a passage's interpretation. Certain of them are now apparent.

(1) 'The governing authorities' (*exousiai*). We have repeatedly stressed the significance of the Graeco-Roman concept of the State in the Cosmos with regard to this word: The Christian's understanding of this world and its (spiritual-human) powers cannot be defined only in terms of sin and evil, for it is also by these powers that the world is saved from chaos. Likewise, the Christian's relationship to these powers is not to be defined only in terms of liberty and contempt, for the *exousiai* are also God's servants and ministers. The world's order, no less than its disorder, has its roots in a scheme of cosmic proportions which was familiar to the mind of Paul's day. Paul is not imparting to the Romans any of this; it is a conception they shared because they were contemporaries in the Roman Empire which ruled the world and whose affairs were those of the universe.[2]

---

combines the two interpretations in the figure of temple ministers collecting tribute (Num. 18.21). It is not clear, however, that taxation was considered payment 'for services rendered' so much as responsibility toward established order.

[3]The reference of εἰς αὐτὸ τοῦτο is disputed. While some associate the phrase with the verb (Meyer, Kühl, Zahn, Weiss, Althaus), with the meaning that the officials are diligent in the collecting of taxes, we prefer to read it (with Sanday-H., Denney, Moule) as relating to the subject, with the meaning that the State is diligent in fulfilling its appointed function, which is much broader than collecting taxes. While Zahn objects that προσκαρτεροῦντες is not appropriate to the idea of fulfilling an office, see otherwise Liddell-S.; Sanday-H. observes that προσκ. cannot be immediately associated with εἰς αὐτὸ τοῦτο, for it always takes the dative (12.13).

[1]It is not clear how specific these terms are. They may refer to tribute and ordinary taxes (Sanday-H., Kirk) or to direct and indirect taxes (Lietzmann, Kühl, Garvie, Findlay); there was perhaps no special distinction intended (Knox).

[2]Very little has been said with regard to the Jewish concept of folk angels since the first chapters because it has little relevance to the circumstance of Paul's writing to Rome. (1) The folk angel concept is a modification and

The Powers That Be

Indispensable as this understanding of *exousiai* is for comprehending Paul's communication, it may not be sufficient for proper exegesis. While it is generally safe to assume that Paul agrees with the prevailing view of things unless he explicitly takes exception to it, proper use of this rule requires careful identification of all that was common to Paul and his Roman readers. In addition to what they shared with their contemporaries, Paul and his readers also held much in common which was distinctively Christian. Paul would not be likely to comment on either of these channels of communication when writing to a church unless he wished to take exception to the prevailing common view or to impart something with regard to a particular aspect of the Christian faith.

Does what Paul imparts in Romans 13.1–7 assume a distinctively Christian understanding of the *exousiai*? At this point it is well to recall that the early Christian faith in Christ as Lord over all things was precisely the kind of redefinition of the prevailing view which was typical of Paul and early Christians.[1] Furthermore, this creed is of particular importance because of its centrality in the early Church and the fact that the realm of Christ's lordship was commonly defined in terms of the principalities and powers.[2] These powers appear to be as integral to early Christian formulation of the gospel as to the contemporary view of the world. If early Christians accepted the prevailing view that the State shared in the structure of things, how were they to conceive of the *exousiai*? This was not an optional question, but one raised by the world in which they lived. There is no alternative to the conclu-

---

special form of a belief which was much more common in other terms, as has been shown above in reference to the Graeco-Roman belief in power, astrology, monotheism, and *daimones* (pp. 75–90). (2) The kind of nationalism which made the folk angel concept of significance to Judaism had very little meaning in the Graeco-Roman world; the period generally was more to be characterized by individualism than nationalism (pp. 69 f.) (3) We do not know if Paul was introduced to the broader conception through the Jewish folk angel doctrine, but there is no evidence in any of Paul's letters that the nationalistic elements distinguishing the Jewish conception were of any significance. Quite otherwise, Paul appears to abandon the idea that any significance is to be attributed to nationalistic distinctions, especially between Jew and Gentile. Whatever distinction may have existed was abolished in Christ.

[1] Cf. above pp. 84-88.
[2] Cf. pp. 28. f.

sion that Christians thought of the *exousiai* as they did of all cosmic powers, from a distinctively Christian point of view.

Underlying what Paul imparted concerning the *exousiai* is a point of view compounded of the contemporary concept of the State as amended by the distinctive faith in Christ. Both the cosmic context of the State and the lordship of Christ are factors for communication in Romans 13.1-7. Although Paul is imparting nothing to the Romans on either subject, for they were concepts shared by Christians in his day, we can ignore them only at the price of failing to share in his communication.

(2) The appointed[1] servants and ministers. One feature of cosmic rule which was evident in the organization of civil government was the hierarchy of authority; superiors and subordinates, both spiritual and human, were part of the order of things. We have seen that their designation as 'servants' and 'ministers' was common.[2] The real question in Paul's day was not so much concerning the *order* of the Cosmos—that was everywhere evident where Rome ruled or where men speculated about the stars or employed magic or had religious or philosophical hope or despair—but the great question was with regard to the *end and meaning* of the cosmic order and its relationship to a host of private lives with their hopes and fears. That the universe and all its powers were knit into an order was only half the answer; the other half was the quest of the age, and men associated themselves into societies, sects, and schools as they believed they found the answer. It was into this world that the early Church went preaching the good news which was the other half of the answer; Jesus Christ is Lord. It was *for him* that 'all things were created in heaven and on earth, visible and invisible, whether thrones or dominions or principalities or authorities—all things were created through him and for him. He is before all things, and in him all things hold together' (Col. 1.16 f.). Christ was the answer to the search for meaning, direction, and hope. The Graeco-Roman world required an answer in cosmic terms, and Christians responded by setting their faith in reference to the powers. The world order *from creation* had been for Christ, and it had its very structure in

---

[1] Cf. the force of this concept in vv. 1 and 2: ὑποτάσσω, τεταγμέναι, ἀντιτασσόμενος, διαταγῇ.

[2] Cf. above, e.g. pp. 79, 82, 84 n. 6, 92 n. 2, 95-97 and 108 n. 3 above.

him. That the governing authorities were servants of *God* is by no means a non-Christological statement. As surely as the readers of Romans understood the State as an ordered 'servant' because of the widespread world view, they would understand 'God' as Christians, in no anaemic isolation from the centre of redemptive activity and the larger answer to the Graeco-Roman quest.

(3) 'By God.' We have seen that the Graeco-Roman notion of powers in the Cosmos was integral to various ideas of monotheistic world order which made the prevailing world view more readily adaptable to Jewish and Christian thought. In light of this, Paul's reference to God *six times* in our passage is not without significance. He does not attack the prevailing view of the cosmic order or the place of the State in it any more than he elsewhere challenges the existence of demons and other spiritual creatures, but by subordinating the governing authorities to God, Paul's statement is of theological importance for the early Church.

While his *words* might well have been imparted by a Rabbi or philosopher,[1] this does not mean that one can enter into communication with *Paul* on the subject of the State without keeping in the foreground his faith in Christ as the one in whom and for whom God created all things. The early Christian confession of Christ as Lord was not just an affirmation of personal allegiance, but a conviction with regard to the purpose of God, the present order of things, and their sure destination. Christology was not a self-contained supplement to a standard theology, but the central point from which Paul comprehended the whole of God's revealed plan.[2] Therefore, we must challenge the common observation that our passage contains 'nothing distinctively Christian' or the supposition that 'God' here is either a neutral reference to 'divinity' or of rabbinical significance. Paul's repeated subordination of the political order to God indicates that he is speaking theologically. He imparts nothing to his readers concerning this God or his purpose, for it is an understanding shared by writer and readers, yet until we take into account the significance of Christ in Paul's understanding of God, we shall fail to share in this communication.

[1] Cf. p. 103 n. 2 above.
[2] This is well established by the *Heilsgeschichte* school. Cf. Cullmann's *Christology* and pp. 28 f. above.

The Powers That Be

(4) 'Be subject.' The preceding chapter indicates that subjection to authorities was not merely a 'political' disposition, but was directly related to one's view of the world order. It was this association which proved Stoicism a politically favourable system, while the new religions, especially those which considered the cosmic order diabolical and sought freedom from the oppressive powers, became politically suspect. It is no accident that Paul made his exhortation to civil obedience in terms of God's order; subjection to authorities required a cosmic understanding.

But Paul imparts nothing here either with regard to the nature of the Cosmos or the Christian faith. Yet the very structure of the contemporary thought meant that any exhortation to be subject to the State would necessarily raise a theological question for Christians. 'If with Christ you died to the elemental spirits of the universe, why do you live as if you still belonged to the world? Why do you submit to regulations?' (Col. 2.20). No longer[1] can it be held that a point of view which raises such a question must be invalid, for this question arises not from a theological hypothesis, but from the encounter of the central creed of the Church with the contemporary world view. This question underlies the problem of Christian insubordination and suggests the reason why Paul wrote what he did in Romans 13. Subjection raised a theological problem for the Christian for the same reason that the gospel raised the question of civil disobedience in the minds of magistrates.[2] This is why it is improper for us to neglect the common faith shared by Paul and his readers in the exegesis of our passage.

The very factors which chapter IV indicated as essential to the communication of our passage now implicate the early Christian faith as no less a factor for our exegesis. This is not to say that Paul was consciously reflecting on these things as he composed his letter, any more than that he intended to impart something about them to Rome, but it is certain that we, who are now quite remote from the original conditions, cannot grasp what Paul was

---

[1] Cf. pp. 45 f., 53 f., where the idea of 'recommissioning of powers' is rightly opposed but on the false assumption that subjection to the State in no way involved the Christian with powers.

[2] Cf. above p. 85.

communicating without keeping before us what was so common to Christian thought at the time that it could be assumed.

THE THEOLOGICAL CONTEXT OF THE COMMUNICATION

It remains for us to summarize and examine our interpretation of Romans 13.1–7 in the light of Paul's view of (*a*) Christ and the *exousiai*, and (*b*) the Christian and the *exousiai*.

Christ and the Exousiai

To ask about Paul's view of the State in Romans 13.1–7 is to ask about his understanding of civil authorities as the servants of God in the period of Christ's lordship. Our study up to this point indicates that we cannot grasp Paul's thought in this regard until we have considered the relationship between Christ and the *exousiai*. Paul's frequent formulation of the gospel in terms of Christ's victory and lordship over the spiritual powers raises a number of questions when placed against the background of contemporary views of the State.

(1) If civil authorities and spiritual powers are intimately associated in Graeco-Roman thought, what is the nature of a victory over the spiritual powers which, to all appearances, makes no significant change whatever in the character or policy of the civil authorities?

Following the pattern of the early *kerygma*, the Church has variously conceived of Christ's work as an event with objectively valid consequences. Propitiation, ransom, victory over sin, death and the spiritual powers, etc. were acclaimed realities in themselves, while the human role in redemption was limited to a subjective appropriation of these benefits by faith (and this, of course, contingent upon election and the work of the Holy Spirit).[1] In recent years, following the heyday of *Religionsgeschichte*

[1] Barth refers to an *objective* reality which must be *subjectively* received: 'When we say justification, sanctification and calling, on the one side we are already expounding the relevance of what was done in Jesus Christ, but, on the other, we are expounding only the objective relevance of it and not its subjective apprehension and acceptance in the world and by us men. . . . In the Christian there is an approbation of the grace of God ascribed to all men in Jesus Christ, a subjective apprehension of what has been done for the whole world in the happening of atonement. It is absolutely and exclusively in the being and work of Jesus Christ Himself and not in men that this specific form of grace has its basis and power. . . . To that extent, objectively, all are justified, sanctified and called. But the hand of God has not

The Powers That Be

and the recovery of the 'classical view' of the atonement (Aulén), the spiritual powers have played an increasingly significant role in attesting the objective character of Christ's work. When the new interpretation of Romans 13.1-7 (cf. ch. I) showed the State to be subject to these powers, and therefore in a special relationship to Christ, portrayal of the objective consequences of Christ's work entered a new dimension. *However, the governing authorities were not affected.* Rome was no different the week after the resurrection from what it was the week before it. In the light of the ancient principle of correspondence in the Cosmos, the statement that Christ defeated the *exousiai* appears to contradict all the evidence.[1]

The only way of explaining this situation to our modern 'logic' lies in the understanding that the cosmic formulation of the work of Christ is not a 'different gospel' from the other formulations which speak of his victory over sin and death. At the same time that the early Church proclaimed Christ's victory over the forces of darkness and evil, it never denied their existence or failed to take seriously their continuing authority and effectiveness in the world.[2] For this reason, we have to do with no ordinary question of 'objectivity'. Although subjective appropriation of objective truth seems to account for the fact that Christians alone benefit from justification,[3] once civil authorities are shown to be co-ordinated with cosmic rule and to bear the name *exousiai*, then the

---

touched all in such a way that they can see and hear, perceive and accept and receive all that God is for all and therefore for them, how therefore they can exist and think and live. To those who have not been touched in this way by the hand of God the axiom that Jesus Christ is the Victor is as such unknown. It is a Christian and not a general axiom; valid generally, but not generally observed and acknowledged.' CD IV/1, 147 f. (§ 58, 4: Survey of the Doctrine of Reconciliation).

[1] Cf. pp. 17-20, 70-99 on the general principles, and note (e.g. pp. 72, 78 n. 1, 79 n. 4, 82, 98 f.) the distinctive role of the State in defining the status of things in the spiritual world.

[2] The rule of sin and death (Rom. 5.12-21) is broken in such a way that they themselves (1 Cor. 15.26; Rom. 6.9; Gal. 5.1) are not restrained, but Christians become victors over both sin and death in Christ (Rom. 6.3-5; 8.2; Col. 2.12 f.). Cf. below the discussion of the victory over the powers in Paul.

[3] The benefits of Christ's work are regularly contingent upon hearing the gospel and believing: Rom. 3.22; I Cor. 1.21; cf. Rom. 1.16; 10.9 ff.; I Cor. 1.18 ff. Bultmann's criticism of the *heilsgeschichtlich* theology (cf. 'Heilsgeschichte und Geschichte' [see p. 40], pp. 662-6) tends to err in the other extreme, however, and so it must be insisted that there can be no definition

oversimplification is exposed. When we call the emperor forth to view his new Christological clothes in broad daylight, we find that there are none, and if the emperor has none, then the *exousiai* have none, and if the *exousiai* have none, then we may suspect that we cannot consider the spiritual powers, any more than the governing authorities or sin or death, as simple objects of Christ's work. The more we consider the matter, the more evident it becomes that the *exousiai* have not been transformed in their character or affected in their hold upon 'this world'; they were not the objects of God's work in Christ.

(2) What then are we to make of the repeated declaration of Christ's victory over the powers? It is helpful in this regard to consider the passages in which Paul speaks of the powers. First, we may mention those which indicate that the powers are still at large. I Cor. 15.24, 25, 28 define the period of Christ's lordship precisely as the time of his conflict with the powers. Eph. 6.12 indicates that Christians are engaged in this conflict. I Cor. 2.6 observes that the powers are destined to lose their dominion, but implies that they have not lost it yet (cf. Gal. 4.8 f.).

Now we may consider those passages which in one way or another refer to Christ's victory or the powers' defeat. Col. 2.15 is typical: '(God) disarmed the principalities and powers and made a public example of them, triumphing over them in (Christ)'. In the section, beginning with v. 8, Paul opposes Christian subjection to 'the elemental spirits of the universe' rather than to Christ. He states his case by showing how *'you have come to fullness of life in him, who is the head of every principality and authority'* v. 10). That is, he sets forth not what has happened to the powers, but what has happened to Christians in Christ (συνταφέντες, συνηγέρθητε, συνεζωοποίησεν). The significance of v. 15 is explained forthrightly in v. 20: *'you* died with Christ to the elemental spirits . . . .';[1] it was not the spirits who were affected, but the believers.

---

of the work of Christ simply in terms of 'redemptive event' apart from the first historic act. The historic act is primary and basic, and for the New Testament, if not for Bultmann, this includes the resurrection and exaltation of Christ.

[1]Cf. Rom. 7.4, 6 where Paul breaks the analogy of vv. 1-3. He cannot say that the Law has died, for as a matter of fact, it is quite alive. Rather, it is the Christian's relationship to the Law which has been altered by a change in the Christian.

The Powers That Be

Likewise, 'you have been raised (συνηγέρθητε) with Christ . . . for you have died and your life is hid with Christ in God' (3.1, 3). In 3.5 ff. it is evident that not only are the powers still at large and effective among the 'sons of disobedience', but the Christian too sojourns in the sphere of their influence, in this age before the appearance of Christ. Paul's argument is not based upon instruction in the nature of the cosmic order, for that was not the locus of Christ's victory, but he spoke of the significance of Christ for those who 'received Christ Jesus the Lord' (2.6). Col. 2.15 then is not a statement concerning the powers *per se*, but the Christian's relationship to the powers.

Eph. 1.21 is similar. Paul's statement of Christ's supremacy over the powers is not so much a description of a general 'objective' cosmic event as the portrayal of his work on behalf of Christians,[1] for he 'made us alive together (συνεζωοποίησεν) with Christ and raised us up with him (συνήγειρεν) and *made us to sit with him* (συνεκάθισεν) *in the heavenly places*' (2.5 f.). For Paul, the significance of Christ's victory is found among those who believe. In 2.1 ff. we see clearly the nature of this victory. It is not that something has happened to the principalities and powers, for 'the prince of the power (ἐξουσία) of the air' is even at this present time at work among 'the sons of disobedience' (2.2 f.). Rather it is that the love of God in Christ has effectively delivered those who believe from the dominion of trespasses and sins (2.1, 4). The locus of Christ's victory is the Church.

The triumphant conclusion to Romans 8 confirms this point of view: the persuasion that 'we are more than conquerors' rests not in a description of the condition of the powers, but in Christ's assurance that God 'will . . . also give us all things in him'. Consequently, the mission of the Church to proclaim Christ is at once the means whereby God's work in Christ may become effective among all men (cf. e.g. Eph. 3.8–11[2]) and the means of bringing the powers to nothing (Eph. 6.17 b).

[1] Cf. εἰς ἡμᾶς (v. 19) and τῇ ἐκκλησίᾳ (v. 22).
[2] That Eph. 3.10 means the 'redemption' of the powers as well is doubtful, but cf. Col. 1.20 with I Cor. 2.6; 15.24. In any case, apocalyptic tradition is divided on the final disposition of evil forces. Cf. the lion as a symbol in the OT: in some traditions, there will be no lions in the new earth (Isa. 35.9); in others there will be lions, but they will lose their lion-like characteristics (Isa. 11.6 f.). Cf. G. B. Caird, *Principalities and Powers*, Oxford, 1954, p. 83.

Paul's reference to the στοιχεῖα ('elemental spirits') strikingly supports our observation. These powers were appointed to guardianship over men by God (Gal. 4.3; cf. 3.23 f.). At the proper time, Christians were released from this 'slavery' by the sending of God's Son and his Spirit (Gal. 4.4–7). The decisive event changed the believers' status: they became sons and heirs of God. It did not change the character or impair the effectiveness of the powers, however, for they were yet able to rule in the sphere of ignorance and even to threaten Christian freedom (Gal. 4.9; Col. 2.20). Far from believing that the powers were subdued or converted, Paul insisted that Christians beware of the powers (Col. 2.8; Eph. 6.18) and take as their defence the faith by which they attained their freedom (Gal. 5.1; Eph. 6.11 ff.; Col. 3.1–3).

There now remains[1] Col. 1.16 (cf. 2.10), which declares that Christ is Lord over the principalities and powers from creation.[2] It is only here that Paul states the relationship between Christ and the powers *per se*. There is no question in Paul's mind as to whether Christ is Lord over the powers, but the New Testament will not support the thesis that he became Lord over them as a consequence of his death and resurrection. His work was crucial

[1] Phil. 2.9 does not actually mention the powers by technical terms, but, because of the reference to 'names', it is customarily included among our passages. Verse 10 should be read as a final clause, but there is no reason to think that Paul believed the end to have been realized in this regard (against Cullmann) when it had not in others. The passage must be interpreted in the light of I Cor. 15.25–28.

Likewise τὰ πάντα is frequently used to indicate the powers. Although God created 'all things' (Rom. 11.36, Eph. 3.9) in Christ and for him (I Cor. 8.6; Col. 1.16 f.), they belong to the alienated (Col. 1.20, cf. p. 117 n. 2 above) and sinful (Gal. 3.22) order of things. To effect his redemptive work among men, God would have to do with spiritual powers (Phil. 3.21), and therefore he subjected them to Christ (I Cor. 15.27). This subjection can hardly have been for Christ's benefit or advantage, for 'all things' were created in and for him. It should rather be conceived as a commission: he, who from the beginning had authority over 'all things', was appointed to reconcile men to God, which meant winning *in them* a victory over the powers. Christ's commission is thus the engagement, not the conclusion of conflict, and the confession 'Christ is Lord' is a cry of victory. The period of Christ's lordship, the special redemptive commission in which the Church also serves, comes to a close only when the redemptive work is completed (I Cor. 15.22, 24, 28, cf. Calvin). But now 'we do not yet see everything subjected to him' (Heb. 2.7 f., with Calvin and Héring opposed to Moffatt and RSV which fails even to note its assumption); it is in this age that the battle is to be waged (cf. Heb. 10.12 f.).

[2] Cf. pp. 35 f. above.

The Powers That Be

for the liberation of believers from the powers, but apart from that, the authority and rule in this world continued as before. As the result of his work, however, Christians came to understand that Christ was Lord over all things from the beginning, and his work was not to straighten out the heavenly spheres but to reconcile men to God. Confession of Christ as Lord was not just a testimony to the Christ-event or a saving experience, but was at the same time the confident assertion that the Redeemer has presided over the order of history and will bring it to a triumphant conclusion.

We have now completed the circle, for we observed first of all that the period of Christ's lordship was far from one of the powers' subjection or defeat, but rather the period of conflict with them. In other words, as we went on to demonstrate, Christ's victory did not have its locus among the powers but in the community of believers. Yet this did not mean that the sphere of Christ's lordship was limited to the Church, or that he held authority only over those who shared in his benefits, for from the beginning 'he is the head of every principality and power . . . and in him all things hold together' (Col. 2.10; 1.17).

(3) The third question has already been answered: If Christ's relationship to the powers is not founded upon his redemptive work, then what is its basis and nature? Christ has been head over the powers and all things from creation, and it was not necessary that anything 'happen' before God could use the State to fulfil his purpose.[1] In this regard, Christ's work served only to reveal to the Church a relationship which had been hidden from the ages (Col. 1.16, 26 f.; I Cor. 2.7 f.; Rom. 16.25).

The confessional character of Paul's references to Christ's victory also suggests that we have to do with abbreviated formulations[2] that declare God's mighty saving act and celebrate the grace in which the Christian stands. By their nature, these formulae exclude descriptions of 'the nature of things', even the relationship of all things to Christ. But the believer, perceiving

---

[1] The presentation of this matter by the *Heilsgeschichte* school is quite satisfactory (cf. 'd' above, pp. 35 f.) so long as they do not attempt to impress upon it the notion that everything which was created in Christ was subsequently somehow affected by the Christ-event.

[2] On the confessional and abbreviated character of Paul's references to the powers, cf. Cullmann, *Christology*, pp. 216, 222–5.

that Christ is the source and subject of his freedom and hope, acknowledges Christ as the victor over the powers, which once ruled him and yet dominate the children of wrath. In other words, the very form in which Christ's victory over the powers is cast in the early Christian tradition prohibits our finding in that testimony information about Christ's relationship to all things from the beginning.

We may speak of Christ's subjection of the powers as such only when the lordship of Christ has accomplished its purpose, and a liberated creation is handed over to God (I Cor. 15.28). If from this final act we learn that the Son's significance lies not in relation to God's essence, but to his revelatory action,[1] then his victory tells us not what God has conquered for himself nor of what new sphere he rules, but that those who believe in his love for us are more than conquerors.

(4) Finally, what is the role of the *exousiai*? Paul declared them to be servants in this age when Christ is Lord. But he never designated them servants of Christ; they are always known as servants of God. Why is this? Since 'all things' were created in Christ, there remains no sound basis for eliminating him from Paul's total view of the State's service. Nevertheless, it is quite something else to assert that Paul conceived of the *exousiai* as 'servants of Christ'.

However artificial the orthodox division between the orders of creation and redemption, it does not seem worthy of exegesis to change the terminology of a text for the purpose of modern polemic.[2] It would be far better to enter into the communication itself, allowing the apostle to relate the servants of God to his Christocentric faith. To change Paul's words to read 'servants of Christ' only hinders a proper understanding of his viewpoint.

(*a*) Significant as was the universal lordship of Christ for the early Christians, they associated it with the order of things from creation. The role of governing authorities in the *Heilsgeschichte* depended in no way upon their knowledge of God's revelation or belief in it; they had no essential relationship to what distinguished Christ's work. Because the *exousiai* did not engage in the preaching

[1] Cullmann, *ibid.*, p. 293.
[2] Cf. e.g. pp. 32 f. above.

of the gospel, they did not participate in the service which characterized Christ's mission.

(*b*) On the other hand, there was in the world a community which knew of God's work in Christ, and believed in his love and forgiveness. It was founded upon the work of Christ, and that work had its embodiment in them. But especially this community declared the gospel, and thus uniquely shared in the service for which Christ ruled. When the service of the *exousiai* and the service of the Church are compared, it is immediately evident that one clearly qualifies as the servant of Christ in such a way as to exclude the other.

Paul's view of Christ's universal lordship, i.e., the creation of all things in him and for him, was not an optional accessory to early Christian theology nor a unique dimension for ancient thought; the very character of the Graeco-Roman world view required a cosmic orientation of the Christian faith. It was precisely the isolation of Greek religion from cosmic affairs which made it obsolete in the Hellenistic period.[1] Early Christianity thoughtfully related its faith to history and the cosmic order in the story of *Heilsgeschichte*, and thus proved the gospel meaningful to its time. Yet Christianity began as an act of God, not as a cosmic system. To teach Christ's universal lordship was exposition, not *kerygma*. The gospel dealt rather with the work of Christ, which revealed God's love, forgiveness, and power, the work which wrought victory over sin and death, wrath and powers, in those who believe. For this reason the name of Christ belongs primarily to what came to pass in his work and to those who share in it.

To distinguish between the Church and the State as servant of Christ and servant of God does not mean that one is less necessary to the *Heilsgeschichte*, or that the other has some merit of which to boast, or that they serve two different lords, or tend to separate goals. Yet their services are distinct.[2] The Church serves Christ by engaging in a special mission under his temporary lordship.

---

[1] Cf. pp. 75, 77 above.
[2] Paul's figure of the place of diverse members in one body (I Cor. 12.14–26) could be extended to illustrate the participation of Church and State in one plan. The Church cannot say that it has no need of the State. Rather, the State is shown extra honour by the subjection of Christians to it.

When the mission is accomplished, that service will be discontinued and Christ will resign his office (I Cor. 15.28). The *exousiai* serve God in the State by maintaining order in society. Against the background of Graeco-Roman thought, this was a function of the cosmic order created in Christ. In the light of revelation, the State's service appeared essential to the special mission to which Christ and his Church were appointed. It is not important here to inquire into the eschatological significance of every aspect of civil procedure. The most obvious function has been commonly observed: the State exists to allow the Church to carry out its mission.[1] But the appearance of even the most hostile authorities as instruments of God's will cautions against use of abstract hypotheses to determine the point when the State ceases to serve God. It is much safer to approach the problem from the viewpoint of the Christian's relationship to the governing authorities.

The Christian and the Exousiai

The implications of our distinction between the realm of Christ's authority (all things from the beginning) and the locus of his victory (those who believe) are far-reaching, but we can pursue here only its significance for Paul's view of the Christians' relationship to civil authorities.

God's work in Christ meant to the early Church the radical reorientation of the believer's existence in the world. They expressed this as resurrection with Christ from the dead, sitting with him in the heavenly places, or being born again. Yet what they confessed as Christ's work was not merely an inner feeling or a new idea but was incarnate in the *ecclesia*. Outside the Church it was not only unknown but without consequence. Therefore, entering into the benefits of Christ's work by faith was inconceivable apart from entering into the realm of its realization. The radical reorientation, which is at once life in Christ and incorporation into his body, determines the Christian's relationship to his fellow man as well as to the realm of his existence. A person may become the object of another's love, not because he has become lovable, but because the other has been enabled to love him. The world of natural and social forces may lose its power to hold a man in anxiety, fear, and dependence, not because it has itself lost

[1] Cf. pp. 38 f. above and 124 ff. below.

power, or has been in any way altered, but because that man has found security apart from their authority, and has become free from their domination.[1]

If the Christian's existence has been radically reoriented by the act of God in which he has faith, it is decisive for his relationship to the *exousiai*. This is not merely a psychological deduction, but the basis of frequent Pauline exhortations.[2] Of what significance is the Christian's faith for his relationship to the governing officials?

(1) Christian subjection as relationship in faith.—For Paul, Christian subjection to civil authority was not merely a matter of census statistics and tax receipts, of knowing the rules and system of government and staying out of trouble. The fact that Christ's victory over the *exousiai* has its locus in the Christian, and does not affect the cosmic order, transform the powers, or convert politicians, means that *subjection to the* exousiai *as a Christian is absolutely contingent upon a conscious relationship to governing officials as a man in Christ*.

It is this 'bringing into self-consciousness' in the face of practical questions of Christian relationship to one's fellow men or

---

[1] Note that Epictetus, who shared in the same common world view as did Paul, likewise did not consider the human problem to lie in the order of things, which was divinely established (*Dis.* 2.14.23 ff., cf. 3.15.14). Not even death, exile, tyranny or slavery were thought to be the principal problems, but a person's attitude toward them (1.11.33; 1.29.60; 2.1.13; 3.26.38 f.; *Ench.* 5). That is, the difficulty is within men (*Dis.* 1.12.22 f.; 4.4.32; 3.20.1; 4.1.85–89; 4.4.15), and it is best described as their dependent relationship to persons and things outside themselves (4.1.46 f.) which are thus able to exercise control over them (2.2.26; *Ench.* 14.2). Freedom can be had only by eliminating this reliance on externals and destroying the underlying desires (*Dis.* 4.1.175) and fears, esp. of death (2.18.29 f.; cf. 2.1.38 f.; 3.26.38 f.; 4.1.172). This conquest of inner fear and insecurity can be had by reliance upon God alone (2.16.45–47). This philosophy does not result in civil disobedience, however, for kings are to be obeyed within the sphere of their authority (1.29.9 ff.). Yet the philosopher remains free from any undue reliance upon rulers and aristocrats for his security (a favourite illustration of Epictetus, 1.29.1 ff., 22 ff.), while those who seek such political favour are considered slaves (4.1.6 ff., 46–50, 60–61). It is knowledge of one's own proper place in the world order (as well as actually practising such an understanding!) which allows the philosopher to be at once perfectly submissive to civil authority while he has no anxiety or fear toward it (4.5.34; 4.7.28 ff.).

[2] Cf. e.g. Col. 2.6–3.17; Rom. 6.1–15, Gal. 3.23–4.10; and note on the larger scale the basis for 'therefore' in Rom. 12.1; Eph. 4.1.

environment which prompts some of Paul's most profound theological statements.[1] The basic danger in any relationship of the Christian, including subjection to the State, is the failure to grasp, retain, or keep central in his understanding of himself the significance of his life in Christ. Why is this?

The Christ-event is effectively beneficial only to believers and does not alter external structures directly because it is essentially God's *revelation*. Far from being a magical transforming work, the New Testament acts of God set forth what the Church believes to be the sure signs of his love, forgiveness, and power, revealed to reconcile men to God, and thus to deliver them from the grip of forces which reign in their anxious, guilty, and insecure isolation from him. By their nature, love and forgiveness mean nothing unless they are believed, and reconciliation to God means nothing unless it is, in John's words, an abiding in him. If it is by faith alone that God's grace in Christ becomes effective in the believer, and if Christ's victory over the powers is not to be found elsewhere than within the Church, it is obvious that the Christian's relationship to the *exousiai* depends decidedly upon that vital and continuing relationship to God which is faith and life in Christ. It is for this reason that failure of faith in the Christian means both his falling under the domination of the powers (Galatians and Colossians) and the rendering of Christ's work fruitless for him (II Cor. 6.1; Gal. 4.11; 5.4). Faith in Christ makes known and confirms the conviction that believers are more than conquerors of the spiritual powers (Rom. 8.31–39); why should they be subject to *exousiai*?

(*2*) *Subjection for conscience' sake.*—Our study has indicated that civil officials were intimately associated with spiritual powers in ancient thought, and from that point of view, subjection to one was neither distinguishable from nor preferable to subjection to the other. Furthermore, we have observed that the work of God in Christ did not alter the character or function of the *exousiai*, so there is no special basis for commending them. Whatever grounds Paul had for counselling Christian subjection to the *exousiai* must be found in the nature of the cosmic-civil structure as such, especially as illuminated by revelation.

---

[1] E.g. cf. passages in the previous note as well as I Cor. 6.1–8; 8.1–6; 12.1–3.

The Powers That Be

However distinctly Christian Paul's own viewpoint, his counsel of subjection was not novel, but common to Christians, Jews, and many pagans; the prevailing cosmology was a dominant factor in this agreement. Since the State was part of the cosmic order established by the Ruler of All (however variously conceived), the ancients considered subjection to the State a religious duty, and anarchy was synonymous with atheism. Wise and godly men had no alternative but submission to this order, and no doubt the Christian conscience was largely tempered by this common understanding.

But the early Church also held distinctive views of the order in which the State participated. When the Christian acknowledged the State as the servant of God, he indicated not so much his faith in cosmic order—which was everywhere assumed—as his conviction with regard to the end and purpose of the order in which the State participated.[1] The Church understood the State, therefore, in relation to its own mission in the world, i.e., eschatologically.[2] For this reason, co-operation with the *exousiai* in the fulfilment of their calling was not merely staying out of trouble or adjusting to the cosmic order, but supporting that purpose for which the Christian himself worked in quite a different way. The Christian's being in Christ so informed his understanding, defined his responsibility, and related him to the world in which he lived that he was subject to the *exousiai* 'for conscience' sake'.[3]

From this perspective, it is evident that Paul's exhortation to subjection was founded upon the very ground which was most likely to foster an independent disregard of civil authority. The

---

[1] Prov. 16.9; Rom. 9.17, cf. p. 36 above.
[2] Cf. above pp. 34 f., 106 f., 120 ff.
[3] 'Conscience' in Paul's usage can hardly be distinguished from its meaning in popular Stoic philosophy; Christians were not unique in their obedience to civil authority on grounds of conscience. Paul recognized all sorts of behaviour as conscientious, whether or not it was informed by revelation (Rom. 2.15) or worthy of Christians (I Cor. 10.25 ff.). Yet it is important to note that Paul so closely associates conscience with the self in its actual living responsibility that he forbids offence to a brother's conscience (as a sin against Christ), however much he feels it is misdirected or weak (I Cor. 8.7 ff.). It is precisely this relationship of conscience and the self which enables Paul in Rom. 14 to use 'faith' much as he uses 'conscience' in I Cor. 8 and 10 (cf. Bultmann, *Theology* I, 220). This striking equivalence seems to indicate that being in Christ is a decisive factor for Christian conscience and thus for relationship to the State.

ancients no less than modern critics have sensed something offensive in the subjection of those who are more than conquerors to the *exousiai*. But Paul indicates that it is rather quite appropriate to the servants of Christ that in their earthly ministry they too should for a while remain 'a little lower than the angels'.[1]

While it was well within God's power to invade human history, remove its rulers, destroy the wicked, and establish justice and peace—and this apocalyptic hope was alive in Paul's time—Paul knew that what had taken place in Christ, and thus far characterized his rule, was of a completely different sort. If the consummation of God's purpose was to come through the lordship which had been given to *Christ*, it would not be by binding, converting, or eliminating the powers, but by a work among men. If *Christ's conquest* does not come about *in men*, it does not come about at all! For this reason, the Word became flesh, and the Church was ordained to preach the gospel among men. The Church was no mere 'information service' reporting changes in the cosmic organization, but its word was God's power for salvation.[2] According to God's plan, the powers of this age were to be engaged in conflict by the gospel and were to be defeated through faith.[3] The calling to serve Christ required the Church to live in the sphere of the *exousiai* (Phil. 1.23–25), lower than the 'angels', and dependent upon them for peace and order to accomplish its work. Paul understood that the circumstances of the Church's mission in this world made it impossible for the Church to go it alone. *The work of redemption, even the proclamation of Christ,*

---

[1] Cf. Heb. 2.8 f., I Cor. 6.1–3, ?11.10 and p. 121 n. 2 above.

[2] Rom. 1.16; 10.6–15; I Cor. 1.18, 24; Eph. 6.17. Luther puts it well: 'It is not enough, nor is it Christian, to preach the works, life, and words of Christ as historical facts. . . . Rather ought Christ to be preached to the end that faith in Him may be established, that He may not only be Christ, but be Christ for thee and for me, and that what is said of Him and what His Name denotes may be effectual in us. . . . For death is swallowed up not only in the victory of Christ, but also by our victory, because through faith His victory has become ours, and in that faith we also are conquerors' ('On Christian Liberty', *Works of Martin Luther*, Philadelphia, 1915–32, II, 326 f.).

[3] Again Luther: 'Nor was Christ sent into the world for any other ministry but that of the Word, and the whole spiritual estate, apostles, bishops and all the priests, has been called and instituted only for the ministry of the Word. . . . For God our Father has made all things depend on faith, so that whoever has faith, shall have all and whoever has it not, shall have nothing' (*ibid*, II, 314 f., 318). Cf. Schlier and Schweitzer, pp. 33 n. 1 and 45 n. 5 above.

The Powers That Be

cannot be defined in terms of the Church alone, but only in terms of the Church and the State.[1]

To this we should add that Christian subjection to civil authority is also an act of love toward one's neighbour, for the State does not exist to govern the Church—the *ecclesia* should have a deeper source of peace (cf. I Cor. 6.1–8)—but to protect those who live under the rule of wrath from one another.[2] By subjection to the State, that it may fulfil its service to God in the *Heilsgeschichte* and preserve his neighbour from malice, the Christian man shows in one way that he is 'a perfectly dutiful servant of all, subject to all'. But that is not the whole of it.

(*3*) *Christian freedom from the* exousiai.—Christians shared with their contemporaries not only the idea of the State's role in the cosmic order, but also the awareness that there were more wills and motives at work upon and within governmental officials than that of the Universal Ruler.[3] No wise or godly person (as defined by Stoic, Jew, or Christian) could afford to be subject to the *exousiai* without cautious reflection. The opportunity of using public office for personal gain naturally enough led to the claim of divine sanction for the officials' private enterprise; the ultimate in this direction was the emperor's claim to deity.

Christian subjection to governing authorities 'for conscience' sake' has another side to it. Not from fear of death, or desire for privilege, or any other form of external pressure, is the Christian subject to the State. As a man in Christ, neither life nor death, nor *exousiai* are able to usurp God's rule over him; he is free from the principalities and powers.[4]

The Christian conscience ought to be free not only from the pressure of external authorities and internal fears, but likewise from that of 'eternal principles'. These last are no less instruments of the *exousiai* than the others.[5] It is always at the point where the

---

[1] Cf. above, pp. 37–39.
[2] Rom. 1.28 ff.; Gal. 5.15. Cf. Strack-B, III, 304; Luther, 'Secular Authority', sections IV and V, *Works*, III, 236–41.
[3] Cf. pp. 27 f., 71 f. above.
[4] Rom. 8.35 ff. Cf. Epictetus, *Dis.* 3.22.94 f.: The conscience (συνειδός) of the Cynic is paralleled to the authority which kings exercise by force. Cf. also p. 123 n. 1 above.
[5] G. B. Shaw observes: 'You will never find an Englishman in the wrong. He does everything on principle. He fights you on patriotic principles; he robs you on business principles; he enslaves you on imperial principles' (*Man of Destiny*).

relationship between the Christian and the State is reduced to some principle that the Christian again falls prey to principalities.

As it is for conscience' sake that the Christian is subject to the *exousiai*, so it is for conscience' sake when he asserts his freedom from them. Although submission to governing authorities as servants of God characterizes the ordinary relationship between the Christian and the State, and exceptions are as difficult to define as they are infrequent, it should be remembered that the Christian's relationship to the *exousiai* is not limited to civil matters. To live in this world as a Christian necessarily involves a conscious acquaintance with the principalities and powers which superintend every aspect of human life. The Christian life required Paul and his brethren daily to make decisions regarding their relationship to the powers of this age. Although his relationship to the State brought the Christian into contact with the *exousiai* in their most awful and majestic form, it rested on the same basis as his everyday life, the mature manhood in Christ. As a man in Christ, his conscience alone would determine his subjection to the State or his non-compliance with its demands.

Exception to the Christian's responsibility to be subject to the *exousiai* is only a question of non-compliance for conscience' sake. Exception was not construed as an opportunity for the Christian to burst his bonds and have things the way he always wanted them. Rather, it was contemplated as the occasion in his relationship to the State when circumstances would require him to suffer for his faith. Freedom from the *exousiai*, the estate of the Christian man as 'a perfectly free lord of all subject to none', was never for Paul a way of self-indulgence or personal gain; it was a way of service (II Cor. 11.23 ff.; 1.5–7; Col. 1.24). The nature of the age in which they lived and the character of their calling boded occasions when early Christians must 'obey God rather than men' and suffer (Acts 5.29; 4.19; 14.22; Matt. 24.8 f.). But Paul leaves no doubt whatever that the primary thing is the fulfilment of the Christian's calling, obedient service to Christ. This may be expected to lead to suffering, at times for civil disobedience. But nowhere does non-compliance, or even suffering for that matter, possess any merit of its own. While the Church had no reason to live in fear of civil officials, it was greatly to the advantage of the Christian mission not to provoke the State needlessly. It was not a question of Christian comfort or avoidance of slander which commended co-operation with magistrates as the 'rule' of Christian behaviour. It was simply a fact that the Church stood to benefit far more from the service of the *exousiai* by avoiding their displeasure wherever possible. The conscience of the man in Christ would detect in each instance the point at which no compromise was possible, but until then, resistance to the authorities was not only foolish and injurious to the mission of the Church, but resistance to what God had appointed.

EPILOGUE

THIS essay has aimed at breaking the stalemate in contemporary discussion of Romans 13.1-7. It has confirmed two important elements of the 'theological exegesis' proposed in chapter I. (*a*) The world view of Paul's day, a strong and significant relationship between civil rulers and spiritual powers, was commonly accepted in Graeco-Roman thought. Far from being a peculiarity of Jewish apocalyptic, this relationship was important in the contemporary view of governmental authority, civil obedience, and 'State religion'.

(*b*) To live in a world so conceived made a theological understanding of the State and one's relationship to it unavoidable, especially for Christians, whose central article of faith was God's work through Christ, the Lord. No modern two-dimensional relationship to civil authority was possible. Furthermore, it is clear that faith and life in Christ were the basis of Christian subjection for conscience' sake. Only being in Christ provided the freedom and confidence for humble obedience or patience in suffering.

Having confirmed these two themes, we should note a number of points in the 'theological exegesis' which our study has proved to be unfounded or erroneous. These are summarized in Appendix C.

In the course of our essay, two other significant points have appeared, one methodological, the other theological. (*a*) It is clearly not enough to interpret an ancient writing merely on the basis of what it is *imparting*; it can be properly understood only by the much more difficult, but more interesting process of entering into the life and thought of the time to participate in the *communication*. This means that while we must always consult indexes and lexicons, their limitations, especially their silence, must be born in mind, and we must carry our inquiry beyond their bounds.

(*b*) Our study has required us to distinguish between the realm of Christ's lordship and the locus of his victory. From what we understand to have been in the mind of Paul's time and the character of his faith, such a distinction is mandatory. What appears to have been the early Christian's relationship to the State calls for a rethinking of the modern version of Christ's victory. This not only has significance for the doctrine of atonement, but is basic to the Church's understanding of its mission in the world.

APPENDIX A

CONCERNING THE RULER-CULT

Oriental and Greek Aspects. McEwan is successful in demonstrating the oriental aspects of the ruler-cult. In the Orient, however, it appears to have been inseparable from the ancient, pre-astrological concept of correspondence between the heavenly council and the human king, and the radical difference between their two spheres in Eastern thought, as shown above (pp. 70 ff., 90 ff.), prohibits the 'deification' of a living man. What was possible in Greece, because the margin between heroic benefactors and gods was so narrow and the boundary so obscure, could not be accomplished in the East, where 'there was little soil for deification of rulers to germinate. . . . In Asia deities either were, or were tending to become, cosmic forces, while their worshippers, unlike the Greeks, remained devoutly religious' (Ferguson, p. 15; cf. Frankfort, *Kingship*, pp. 6–12, contrasting Egyptian and Mesopotamian concepts of the ruler, and 295 ff.). But the Hellenistic period provided the opportunity for a mixture of oriental cult and Greek honours which survived the inherent contradiction of the two traditions for generations, until the logical conclusion of what Ptolemy II brought together (see below) was drawn by Gaius, Nero, and other fanatics. But even McEwan must confess that the rulers of the Assyrians, Chaldeans, Persians, and Seleucids, all of whom enjoyed a ruler-cult, 'were not gods according to their cuneiform titularies' (p. 16). 'There is little in Persian literature from which divine kingship is deducible' (p. 18), yet it was in that tradition that Alexander set the precedent for his successors. The fact that monarchy was an importation into Greece from Macedon (p. 23), while divine kingship was foreign to Macedon (p. 30), does not support a genealogical argument linking deification with the spread of monarchy. The ruler-cult, the idea of correspondence, the conception of the ruler as the earthly deputy of the god of the State, especially as it was adapted by the idea of the king's *daimon*, were Hellenism's inheritance from the East, but when this is placed alongside the elevation of kings in Egypt, and of civil benefactors in Greece, to the rank of god, 'deification' hardly seems appropriate to what was derived from Asia. Cf. W. Foerster in G. Quell and W. Foerster, 'κύριος', *TWNT* III, 1048 f.: The use of 'lord' (*dominus*) with regard to the emperors is one way of measuring the oriental influence upon Graeco-Roman conceptions of the ruler. Lord, as applied to deity in the East, was utterly foreign to western ideas of God, and when the concept of 'lord' was finally accepted as an imperial title, it was apart from an indication of the emperor as god (*ibid.*, p. 1054 [23–27]; cf. Frankfort, *Kingship*, pp. 228, 230, 295 ff., esp. 301 ff.).

'*Deification*' *of the Ruler*. The best example is Alexander, who demanded recognition as divine *in Greece* in 324. The background for such an act is attributed to a combination of things. (*a*) It was natural for the Greeks to consider exceptional men as above the law (Plato, *Laws* IX 875; *Statesman* 297A and 303B), and the 'divinity' of the human soul was especially evident in them. (*b*) As observed above, p. 74 n. 4, Greek religion underwent a secularization whereby both gods and noteworthy citizens received identical honours (Charlesworth, p. 9). Whether he was a god or mortal was of minor significance, for many (later, all) gods were thought once to have been human. It is these possibilities, uniquely Greek, which make the idea of a 'divine man' genuinely Hellenic as distinct from oriental. Cf. Ferguson, pp. 13–15; Nock, 'Religious Developments', p. 481; H. Kleinknecht in H. Kleinknecht et al., 'θεός', *TWNT* III, 68 (24 ff.); (Foerster, 'κύριος', *op. cit.*, pp. 1047 [28]—1048 [8]).

The occasion for the entrance of a genuine conception of a living divine king in Hellenistic times came, according to Ferguson (pp. 16 ff.), from the blending of oriental and Greek elements in the person of Ptolemy II of Egypt. Besides being Pharaoh in Egypt, he and his wife were 'children of the Saviour Gods' from the Greek tradition. The two traditions were distinct. 'The one common factor of the two cults was the god Ptolemy, a single symbol for the profound aspirations of two very different people—of the Egyptians for life after death, and of the Greeks for government according to law' (*ibid.*, p. 19). The significance of forging one idea from two cultures is manifest in the radical claims of the fanatical emperors. Goodenough (*Politics of Philo*, p.

Appendix A

107) also sees the excesses of Gaius to be rooted in this fusion and reflection of the popular rather than the philosophical mind (cf. 109 f., Bréhier, pp. 20, 23).

The Fanatics. The notable examples of interest to us are Gaius and Nero. The excess of the former is clear from his break with Augustan tradition, especially following the cautious Tiberius (Suetonius, *Tiberius* 26 f.), and the reaction against it is evident from the return to tradition by Claudius. Nero's extremes included not only public appearances as certain well known deities, but actual identification with Apollo and Helios (as Gaius was hailed as Jupiter Latiaris). While extravagant titles were used for most emperors, these two clearly carried the oriental cult and the Greek honours to the extremes which were traditionally repulsive to Rome, and attempted to realize personally what was instituted only for official purposes. As their greatest opposition was in Roman aristocracy, so their greatest encouragement was in the provinces, for whom the emperor was the appointed guardian and ruler of the world, and, as such was a power with 'divine' associations (Nock, 'Religious Developments', p. 501; A. Momigliano, 'Nero', *CAH* X, 732 f.).

Qualifications. Extravagant titles and impressive cult practice, which glorified the rulers of this period to an extent that partially obscures the excesses of Gaius and Nero, must be evaluated in the light of contemporary thought and practice. (1) However exalted in their lifetime, the emperors were officially admitted to the status of gods only by an official act of the Senate after their death. Furthermore, no ruler could be assured that merely because he was emperor he would be accorded this honour. It was not automatic or inherent, but was based on the quality of his rule (Nock, 'Religious Developments', p. 488; Charlesworth, p. 28). It is noteworthy that those who so conspicuously grasped the honour while ruling were pointedly denied it after death, as if to negate the claims of their lifetime. While the Senate was far more conservative than the masses, its judgment is of value particularly with regard to our estimate of such imperial institutions as the ruler-cult and the titles born by officials of the government (e.g., *Soter, Euergetes,* etc.). (2) While they could be addressed by their cult names, they spoke as kings, not as gods (with the exceptions noted). (3) Religious worship existed alongside the emperor-cult, and offerings were made to the gods on behalf of the emperors. Likewise, even the most fanatic emperors engaged in sacrifice to the gods. (4) No votive offerings, 'the touchstone of piety in antiquity', were directed to rulers, living or dead, in expectation of supernatural blessings. Special attention should be called to the imperial standards (accompanied by the image of the emperor) in the army (see Nock, 'Religious Developments', p. 484; 'Roman Army', pp. 237-41; Charlesworth, p. 31); there is no indication that their veneration included expectation of supernatural help. (5) Altars and oaths with reference to the Genius of Augustus are not indications of deification, but are the adoption of a private practice in which the life spirit of a man's family was honoured by sacrifice on his birthday (Nock, 'Religious Development', p. 484; see above, p. 89 n. 6). (6) The cult itself made no pretence of being anything but a form for the preservation of loyalty to the emperor. It was clearly public and patriotic, designated not so much to heap divine honours upon the emperor in the Greek fashion as, in the oriental tradition, to recognize in the emperor the appointed and fully empowered ruler of the realm. It was precisely the dominance of the political purpose in the ruler-cult which was its great weakness (Nilsson, 'Problems', p. 256; Charlesworth, pp. 27 f.; Nock, 'Religious Developments', pp. 482, 492, etc.; Tarn, *Hel. Civ.*, p. 279). (7) See above, pp. 83 ff., regarding the contemporary vital conception of the ruler's *daimon*, which carried the understanding that however exalted the emperor may be among men, his cosmic significance is as a deputy of a subordinate deity. It is finally the broad and popular influence of astrology, and of the monotheistic tendency to see the powers of the world ordered in a universal plan, which placed the 'deification' of the emperor in its proper perspective. (Frankfort's discussion of 'Deification of Kings' in Mesopotamia is of striking significance in view of widespread misinterpretation of the practice with regard to the emperor cult of Rome; see *Kingship,* ch. 21, esp. pp. 301 ff.)

Titles and Proskynesis. The two most frequently used titles are *Soter* and *Euergetes.* '*Soter* had a wide range of meaning and emphasis in paganism. It was one thing when used to express the gratitude, or hopes, or promises of a moment, another thing when accorded as a constant epithet. But at all times it denoted the performance of a function and not membership of a class in a

Appendix A

hierarchy of beings' (Nock, 'Soter', pp. 129 f.; cf. Knox, p. 39). This may be illustrated by noting that Germanicus refused to be honoured as *Soter* and *Euergetes* in Alexandria, although he had accepted even higher honours within his own territory. The significance of the honour was not so much in the titles themselves as in the circumstances in which they were used. To be so honoured beyond the bounds of one's jurisdiction might be considered politically ambitious. Hence, one was not a *Soter* as such, but with regard to particular circumstances which were principally political (*ibid.*, Nock, 'Soter', pp. 132, 134). The title *Euergetes* was similarly used as an expression of gratitude to the ruler for his benefits to the people (cf. Luke 22.25 f.; Deissmann, *Light*, p. 253). Far from being titles denoting deity, they were used not only of a monarch, but, from the time of Augustus and later, the Egyptian governor and even some of his subordinates were addressed as *Soter*, *Euergetes*, and by similar titles. The titles are thus very near to the honours paid by the Greeks to men who had served the *polis* well, except that now they are not personal, but, like a uniform, belong to the office. In the period of the empire, the emperor himself, who was charged with divine authority to maintain justice and administer numerous other good works, was particularly the benefactor of the people. Cf. Nock, 'Ruler Cult', pp. 35–40.

Deissman (*Light*, pp. 343 ff., cf. Moulton-M, θεός) has presented a mass of evidence dealing with the ascription of 'god' to emperors by localities in the eastern provinces. Recalling the discussions of Greek thought above, we see that the bestowing of divine honours upon rulers is a remnant of the *polis*-centred religion, which had become something like a university which had lost any attraction for students but had retained its power of bestowing honorary degrees. This mass of material is only the most nominal kind of 'deification', particularly impressive upon inscriptions memorializing state occasions. As Deissmann observes (*Light*, p. 347): 'the adjective θεῖος, "divine", is, like the Latin *divinus*, very common in the sense of "Imperial" throughout the whole Imperial period.' The old Greek religion, centred upon the *polis* and its heroes (divine and human), was utterly inadequate for the new age of universal proportions. Men abandoned it for the oriental religions which had adapted themselves to cosmic dimensions. Consequently Greek religious titles remained adequate only for expressing the esteem of the *polis*, but any one who wanted to consider the *gods* must turn to a different sphere. The religious significance of the emperor was to be comprehended within the oriental system, in which he appeared as the deputy of a subordinate god, holding a vast authority by divine appointment. 'The term Genius implied some power which was more than what was seen; and we must allow that when Augustus accepted the worship of his Genius, this was not just a transparent disguise for direct worship of himself. A Genius or Victoria could be regarded as a supernatural entity. . . . The standards could not be so regarded, nor could rulers, living or dead. No honours could cause either to be taken seriously for what they were not' (Nock, 'Roman Army', p. 241).

The prevailing Roman attitude, well into the period of the empire, was shaped not so much by the religious implications of *proskynesis* as by the feeling that 'kneeling to a mortal is not an act worthy of a free man, though it is characteristic of Persia where men are as slaves to their ruler' (Charlesworth, p. 18). Lucius Vitellius is credited as the first to bring to the act the significance of worship of the emperor as well as subservience to him (Suetonius, *Vitellius* 2.5, cf. Charlesworth, p. 19, for Plutarch's views of the act). 'Generally as time goes on the meanings appear to be two: either prostration before a king as a piece of court-ceremonial, or prostration before something regarded as holy. . . . But there is nothing to show that during the first two centuries of the Principate *proskynesis* was ever regarded, by itself, as a cult-act, though it was certainly looked upon at first as a piece of flattery, degrading to the self-respect of the flatterer, foreign and un-Roman; after the Antonines it apparently became a regular part of court etiquette' (*ibid.*, p. 20). Cf. W. W. Tarns's refutation ('Ruler-Cult and the Daemon') of L. R. Taylor's much cited paper ('The "Proskynesis" and the Hellenistic Ruler-Cult', *JHS* 47, 1927, pp. 53 ff.).

APPENDIX B

BIBLIOGRAPHY TO THE QUESTION OF JEWS IN ROME IN THE GRAECO-ROMAN PERIOD

Ludwig BLAU, 'Early Christian Archaeology from the Jewish Point of View', *HUCA* 3, 1926, 157–214; 'Early Christian Epigraphy Considered from the Jewish Point of View', *HUCA* 1, 1924, 221–37. Franz CUMONT, *The Oriental Religions in Roman Paganism*, Chicago, 1911. Adolf DEISSMANN, *Bible Studies*, ET, Edinburgh, 1901, pp. 269–300. J. B. FREY, 'Les communautés juives à Rome aux premiers temps de l'église', *Recherches de Science Religieuse* 20, 1930, 269–97; *ibid.*, 21, 1931, 129–68; 'Le Judaisme, à Rome aux premiers temps de l'église', *Biblica* 12, 1931, 129–56; 'La question des images chez les juifs à la lumière des récentes découvertes', *ibid.*, 15, 1934, 265–300. Hugo GRESSMANN, 'Jewish Life in Ancient Rome', *Jewish Studies in Memory of Israel Abrahams*, New York, 1927, pp. 170–91. Charles GUIGNEBERT, *The Jewish World in the Time of Jesus*, ET, London, 1939. H. J. LEON, 'The Jewish Catacombs and Inscriptions of Rome: an Account of their Discovery and Subsequent History', *HUCA* 5, 1929, 299–314; 'New Material about the Jews of Ancient Rome', *Jewish Quarterly Review* 20, 1929/31, 301–12. Nikolaus MÜLLER, *Die jüdische Katakombe am Monteverde zu Rom*, Leipzig, 1912. Emil SCHÜRER, *Die Gemeindeverfassung der Juden in Rom in der Kaiserzeit* nach den Inschriften dargestellt, Leipzig, 1879. Hermann VOGELSTEIN, *Rome*, Philadelphia, 1940.

The place of magic in the life of Hellenistic Jews reflects to a great extent the influence of the world about them (esp. the belief in powers, astrology, etc.). Cf. Ludwig Blau, *Das altjüdische Zauberwesen*, Strassburg, 1898, pp. 96 ff.; 'Magic', *Jewish Encyclopaedia* VIII, 255–7; Ludwig Blau and Kaufmann Kohler, 'Abraxas', *ibid.*, I, 129 f.; A. R. S. Kennedy, 'Charms and Amulets (Hebrew)', *ERE* III, 439–41. Goodenough's study in *Jewish Symbols* (see p. 63) is vital for the question of the Hellenization of Judaism in this period.

APPENDIX C

SOME NEGATIVE CONSEQUENCES

INASMUCH as our study in chapter IV has confirmed a clear association of spiritual powers and civil rulers in the common thought of Paul's time, and in chapter V it appears that a responsible interpretation of Romans 13.1–7 must take account of Paul's distinctive faith and understanding as a Christian, it would be well for us to state also some negative consequences of our study for the point of view embodied in chapter I (cf. esp. pp. 28 ff.).

If there is no basis for designating the spiritual powers as the objects of Christ's work, and if his victory has its locus in the believer, there is no place for the unchecked speculation that the powers were 'bound' on a leash, or recommissioned, or lost their evil character as a consequence of Christ's work (cf. pp. 29–34, 45–47, 53 f.).

If it cannot be said that they have become obedient to Christ or discharge any service to him other than what has been their custom from the beginning, then such can hardly be the basis of the Christian's honouring the State or subjection to it for conscience' sake.

Furthermore, it is incomprehensible from the viewpoint of Graeco-Roman thought to hold that the relationship between the powers and the State is only 'so far as they subject themselves to Christ's Kingdom' (pp. 30 f.). The idea that the State can 'fall out of the divine order' presupposes (on hypothetical grounds) some obligation to *obey* Christ as normative for the State. But as a matter of fact, the *exousiai* can hardly be expected to obey one of whom they are quite ignorant. In other words, they have no special relationship to Christ's rule from which to fall.[1]

---

[1]The idea of the 'demonic' State as one which has fallen out of God's service into the devil's is a common one and not confined to those proposing the exegesis in Chapter I. (Besides Cullmann and Stählin [cf. p. 31 n. 3] cf. Dehn, p. 108, Künneth, p. 43, Visser 't Hooft, p. 94.) But the significance given to the word 'demonic' by these men is modern, and their view cannot be supported by either Graeco-Roman or biblical thought; it was precisely

Appendix C

When the *exousiai* are considered the objects of Christ's redemptive work, the distinction between the realm of his authority (all things from the beginning) and the locus of his victory (those who believe) is lost, with the following consequences: (*a*) Creation in Christ and the work of Christ are applied to the same object; apparently either the second was unnecessary or the first inconsequential. (*b*) The cosmic application of Christ's work only demonstrates its failure, for nothing happened to the State or sin and death as such. (*c*) The work of Christ and the eschatological consummation are identically described (by blending Col. 2.15, Phil. 2.9 f., I Cor. 15.28); evidently the first work was ineffective, and the 'once for all' event must be *repeated* as the eschatological triumph (cf. pp. 31 n. 2; 47 f.), or was the latter event to be only a formality?

The objective cosmic interpretation of Christ's work obscures its distinctive characteristics, the meaning of faith, and the mission of the Church. While it is well that 'knowledge' should distinguish the Church from the world in the *heilsgeschichtlich* view, this interpretation is justly criticized[1] where it gives the impression[2] that the work of Christ is a generally realized condition and the life in Christ is little more than an informed awareness.

These negative consequences follow from understanding first the relationship between the spiritual powers and civil government, and therefore secondly that the locus of Christ's work cannot be the cosmic powers, but is the Church.

---

through the *daimones* that the Cosmos was ordered, and a dualism which rules out God's control of evil is foreign to Paul's tradition. It is altogether evident that the *exousiai* are not obedient to Christ, but that is not because they fell out of the divine order. Rather, their ministry and relationship to Christ does not rest upon his work, but upon God's creation in him. Cf. pp. 19 n. 4, 36 n. 3, 49 n. 3 and pp. 83 ff.

[1] Cf. Wendland, p. 34, Perles, p. 398.
[2] Cf. Cullmann, *Königs.* pp. 35, 40; relating to the State, *Time*, p. 204; *Christology*, pp. 228–30.

INDEX OF AUTHORS

Abbott, T. K., 42
Acts of John, 22
Acts of Philip, 22
Althaus, P., 41-44, 49, 104-6, 108, 109
Andres, F., 63, 69, 78 f., 81-84
Angus, S., 63, 77, 81
Apollodorus, 76
Apollonius, 89
Aristides, 89
Athenagoras, 22, 85, 87
Aulén, G., 115

Bachmann, P., 24
Barker, E., 63, 70
Barnabas, 22, 30
Barth, K., 9, 14, 17 f., 25, 29, 31-34, 38 f., 41, 46, 50, 52, 114
Bauer, G., 11, 13
Bauer, W., 26
Bertholet, A., 19
Beza, T., 107
Bieder, W., 17, 25, 28
Blau, L., 138
Bonhoeffer, D., 29, 39
Bornkamm, G., 40, 42 f., 49
Bousset, W., 24 f., 44
Bousset-G., 9, 18 f.
Bréhier, E., 63, 79, 89, 95 f., 133
Brunner, E., 40 f., 44-46, 49, 52-54
Bultmann, R., 17 f., 21, 24, 27, 30, 36, 40 f., 67, 115, 125

Caird, G. B., 117
Calvin, J., 107 f., 118
Campenhausen, H. von, 40-42, 44-51, 57, 103 f.
Cassirer, E., 27
Celsus, 84-87
Charles, R. H., 9, 18 f., 23
Charlesworth, M. P., 63, 91, 93, 132-34, 136
Cheyne, T. K., 19, 34
Cicero, 88 f., 91
Clement, I, 11, 22, 30
Clement, II, 35
Cochrane, C. N., 63, 91
Colson, F. H., 95 f.
Cornely, R., 108
Cornill, C. H., 19
Craig, C. T., 24
Cross, F. M., 20

Cullmann, O., 14, 17, 21, 23-25, 28-36, 38-41, 45 f., 48, 50-52, 112, 118-20, 138 f.
Cumont, F., 63, 77-79, 84, 138

Dehn, G., 11-13, 17, 22-26, 30, 33, 36, 38-40, 43, 57, 138
Deissmann, A., 11, 22, 55, 63, 135, 137
Delling, G., 24, 26, 30, 44
Denney, J., 104, 106-9
Dibelius, M., 11, 13 f., 18-20, 23-25, 27, 30 f., 34 f., 55, 63, 66 f.
Dio Chrysostom, 96
Diogenes Laertius, 75
Diognetus, 35
Diotogenes, 79, 96
Dodd, C. H., 34, 63, 83, 93, 94, 96, 104, 107 f.
Doerne, M., 40 f., 45, 47, 51 f.
Driver, S. R., 19

Eck, O., 40 f.
Ecphantus, 79, 96
Eggenberger, C., 39
Eissfeldt, O., 20
Ellert, W., 40 f.
Enslin, M. S., 65
Epictetus, 123, 127
Everling, O., 24, 44
Ewald, G. H. A., 107

Ferguson, W. S., 63, 68, 81, 91 f., 131 f.
Festugière, A. M. J., 63, 69, 77 f., 83 f.
Feuillet, A., 41
Fichtner, J., 19, 36
Filson, F. V., 63, 66
Findlay, G. G., 25, 104 f., 108 f.
Foerster, W., 26 f., 36, 42, 83, 132
Forsyth, P. T., 31
Frankfort, H. and H. A., 9, 63, 70-72, 88, 131 f., 134
Frey, J. B., 137
Fuchs, H., 40, 69

Garvie, A. E., 104, 107-9
Gaugler, E., 40 f., 44, 49, 53, 103 f., 107 f.

Ginsberg, L., 9, 18 f., 23
Glover, T. R., 63, 80, 83
Godet, F. 24 f., 104, 107
Goodenough, E. R., 63 f., 76, 79, 88, 91, 93, 95-97, 132, 137
Goudge, H. L., 24
Grant, F. C., 64, 69
Gressmann, H., 64, 69, 81, 137
Grundmann, W., 26, 30, 34, 64, 75-77, 94-96
Guignebert, C., 137
Gunkel, H., 20
Gurney, O. R., 70, 73
Gutbrod, W., 91

Heinrici, G. F., 24
Hennecke, E., 9, 18, 24
Héring, J., 40, 45, 52, 54, 118
Hermetica, 83-86, 89
Herodotus, 74
Hesiod, 76
Hofmann, J. C. von, 107 f.
Holtzmann, O., 24, 104
Homer, 89
Hort, F. J. A., 107

Iamblichus, 84
Ignatius, 30
Irenaeus, 30, 48, 50, 58, 65

Jacobsen, T., 70-72
Jacoby, F., 76
Jonas, H., 64, 69, 73, 75, 78
Jones, M., 17 f., 21, 24, 35
Jülicher, A., 104
Justin, 21-23, 30, 46, 85, 87

Kautzsch, E., 9, 19
Kennedy, A. R. S., 137
Kirk, K. E., 109
Kittel, G., 25 f., 36, 40-44, 48, 57
Kleinknecht, H., 91, 132
Klöpper, A., 24
Knox, J., 104 f., 109
Knox, W. L., 64, 74, 96, 133
Koch-Mehrin, J., 40 f.
Kohler, K., 138
Kühl, E., 105-9
Künneth, W., 11 f., 25, 31, 38-41, 52, 102, 138

Lachmann, C., 107

140

Index of Authors

Lagrange, M. J., 19, 104, 107 f.
Leenhardt, F. J., 40, 42, 44–46, 49 f.
Leon, H. J., 137
Lietzmann, H., 24 f., 44, 104, 107 f., 119
Liddell-S., 9, 83, 108 f.
Lohmeyer, E., 27, 45
Luther, M., 107, 126 f.

McEwan, C. W., 64, 71 f., 91 f., 131
Macgregor, G. H. C., 17 f., 21, 24, 27, 30 f., 34, 36
Manson, W., 17, 21, 25
Marcion, 84
Marti, K., 19
Massie, J., 24 f.
Masson, C., 36
Menander, 83
Merlan, P., 85
Meyer, H. A. W., 24 f., 104, 107–9
Meyer, W., 24 f.
Michaelis, W., 80, 94
Michel, O., 41, 49, 104, 106
Moffatt, J., 24 f., 107, 118
Mögling, W., 39
Momigliano, A., 133
Moore, G. F., 9, 18 f.
Morgenthaler, R., 25
Moschopoulous, 76
Moule, H. C. G., 104, 107–9
Moulton-M., 9, 94, 135
Müller, N., 137
Munck, J., 41
Murray, G., 64, 73 f., 77, 82

Nilsson, M. P., 64, 70, 73–79, 81–83, 96, 134
Nock, A. D., 64, 74, 76 f., 79, 81–84, 86, 88–92, 96, 132–6
Nock-F., 10, 83–85
Nygren, A., 41, 52

Oepke, A., 40 f., 44

Origen, 84–87
Owen, E. C. E., 84

Papyri Graeci, Magici, 75, 83
Parry, R. St. J., 24 f., 104, 107 f.
Pearson, A. C., 83, 86
Perles, O., 40 f., 43, 51 f., 102, 139
Peterson, E., 17 f., 28
Philippi, F. A., 107
Philo, 89, 95–97
Philostratus, 89
Plato, 89, 132
Plotinus, 83
Plummer, A., 24 f.
Plutarch, 75, 79 f., 83 f., 89, 93
Polycarp, 11, 13, 23, 30, 34, 39, 48, 65, 107
Porphyry, 84

Rad, G. von, 26
Reicke, B., 17, 20, 22 f., 25 f., 30, 32, 57, 85, 94
Robertson, A., 24 f.
Robinson, H. W., 19
Rose, H. J., 64, 83, 89

Sanday-H., 107–9
Santayana, G., 27
Sasse, H., 27, 64, 78, 87
Schelkle, K. H., 40, 50, 58
Schlatter, A., 24, 44
Schlier, H., 11–13, 17, 21 f., 25, 27, 33–35, 38 f., 43, 126
Schmiedel, P. W., 24 f.
Schmidt, K. L., 11–13, 19, 21 f., 25–27, 35, 38–40, 50, 57, 64, 70, 95
Schniewind, J., 44
Schultz, H., 19
Schürer, E., 10, 137
Schweitzer, A., 66
Schweitzer, W., 17, 24–26, 30–33, 35, 39–47, 50, 52, 54, 61, 126

Scott, C. A., 24
Scott, W., 10, 84
Shaw, G. B., 127
Stade, B., 19
Stählin, G., 31, 36, 40–42, 44
Stauffer, E., 64, 82, 88
Stewart, J., 17, 21, 24, 27, 31, 34
Sthenidas, 96
Strack-B., 10, 18–20, 23 f., 49, 53, 127
Strobel, A., 40, 43 f., 47, 69
Suetonius, 89, 133, 136
Synge, F. C., 36

Tarn, W. W., 64, 70, 78, 81, 86, 89, 91, 134, 136
Tatian, 21
Taylor, L. R., 136
Tholuck, F. A.G., 107 f.
Tischendorf, C. von, 107

Varro, 91
Vischer, L., 12, 45
Visser't Hooft, W. A., 17, 28, 31–33, 138
Vogelstein, H., 137

Waser, O., 64, 74, 83–85, 94
Weiss, B., 24 f., 104, 107, 109
Weiss, J., 44
Wendland, H. D., 17, 25, 27, 34, 36, 39, 43, 48, 52, 102, 139
Wette, W. M. L. de, 108
Whitehouse, W. A., 52
Wieser, G., 41
Williams, G. H., 37
Wilson, J. A., 70–72
Wright, G. E., 20

Young, P., 107

Zahn, T., 104, 107–9

INDEX OF BIBLICAL REFERENCES

Bible Ref.	Page
OLD TESTAMENT	
Genesis	
2.1 LXX	95
6.2	94
Exodus	
22.22–4	96
Leviticus	
7.27	107
17.12	107
Numbers	
6.6	11, 107
18.21	109
Deuteronomy	
4.19	19
4.19 LXX	95
17.3 LXX	95
17.15	104
29.25 ff.	19
32.7 ff. LXX	22
32.8 LXX	18 f., 94
32.17	86
33.2	18
Judges	
5.20	95
Kingdoms	
I–IV LXX	94
II Samuel	
24.16	19
I Chronicles	
LXX	94
Job	
1.6	18
1.6 LXX	22, 94
1–2	19
2.1	18
2.1 LXX	94
5.1	18
15.15	18
Psalms	
LXX	94
8.6 LXX	94
8.7	31
23 LXX	23
24.7	21
29.1	18
34.8	85
58	19
82	19 f., 34
89.6–8	18

Bible Ref.	Page
Psalms—cont.	
95.5 LXX	22 f.
96.5 LXX	94
102.21 LXX	94
106.37	86
110	23, 30, 33
137.1 LXX	94
148.2 f.	94
Proverbs	
16.9	125
Isaiah	
11.6 f.	117
24.21 LXX	95
24.21 ff.	20
30.4 LXX	22
35.9	117
40.26 LXX	95
45.1 ff.	36
45.23	23
65.25	106
Jeremiah	
LXX	94
21.7	49
25.9 ff.	36
29.7	49
Daniel	
2.21	49, 87
2.37 f.	49
3.18	11
3.92(25) LXX	94
4.14 (17)	49
4.28	104
10.13	18, 20
10.20 f.	18, 20
12.1	18, 20
Amos	
LXX	94
4.2 LXX	18
Zechariah	
LXX	94
14.5	18
Minor Prophets	
LXX	94
APOCRYPHA AND PSEUDEPIGRAPHA	
Wisdom	
5.17, 20	95

Bible Ref.	Page
Wisdom—cont.	
6.1–11	49, 104
13.2	95
16.17, 24	95
18.24 f.	95
19.6	95
Ecclesiasticus	
10.4	87
17.17	19
Baruch	
4.27	107
Jubilees	
15.30 ff.	19
15.31	19, 23
Enoch	
1.9	18
6.2	18
46.5	49
89.51 ff.	23
89.59 f.	19
90.20 ff.	19
90.22	23
90.24 f.	25
Ascension of Isaiah	
10.17–11.35	24
NEW TESTAMENT	
Matthew	
8.9	42
9.18, 34	43
18.10	85
24.8 f.	128
Mark	
6.14 ff.	11
10.42	11
12.14	104
12.17	11, 108
13.34	42
15.2	11
Luke	
2.1	11
4.5–8	25
12.11	25, 42 f.
13.32	12
20.25	12
22.25 f.	136
23.2	11
23.13	43

Index of Biblical References

Bible Ref.	Page
John	
1.1 ff.	36
12.31	43
17.24	36
19	52
19.12	11
Acts	
2.33, 36	11
2.43	107
3.23	107
4.1	11
4.19	11, 128
4.25 ff.	30, 36
5.29	11, 128
5.31	11
7.38, 53	23
14.22	128
16.19	43
16.20 f.	105
16.20–24	13
17.6 f.	11
17.7	105
17.22–31	66
18.12 ff.	12
19.38 ff.	12
24.5	11
25.26	22
Romans	
1.16	115, 126
1.18 ff.	83
1.21	66
1.28 ff.	127
2.15	125
3.22	115
5.12–21	115
6.1–15	123
6.3–5	115
6.4	66
6.9	115
6.12	32
6.12 f.	11
7.1–4, 6	116
8	105, 117
8.2	115
8.9	66
8.23	32
8.31–39	124
8.35 f.	13
8.35 ff.	127
8.38	26, 32, 45
9–11	105
9.17	36, 125
10.6–15	126
10.9	11, 66

Bible Ref.	Page
Romans—cont.	
10.9 ff.	115
11.36	118
12	64, 106
12.1	123
12.1 f.	104
12.2	11
12.3	104
12.13	109
12.19	34, 104
13 (1–7)	esp. 25 ff., 104 ff., 107–9, 130
13.1	25, 42 f., 49, 111
13.2	43, 111
13.2–5	39
13.3	26, 43
13.4	12, 33 f.
13.5	108
13.6	12, 33, 46
14	125
15.6	66
16.25	119
16.25 f.	66
I Corinthians	
1.18	126
1.18 ff.	115
1.21	66, 115
1.24	126
2	25
2.6	26, 43, 116 f.
2.6–8	44
2.6–16	66
2.6 ff.	23, 30
2.7 f.	119
2.8	22, 25 f., 29 f., 43 f., 50, 56, 59 f., 61
4.9	13, 23
4.12	13
5.5	83
6	25
6.1 ff.	13, 23 f., 35, 56, 60
6.1–3	126
6.1–8	124, 127
6.4	12
7.30	32
7.37	42
8	125
8.1–6	124
8.4–6	66
8.5	22
8.6	36, 118

Bible Ref.	Page
I Corinthians—cont.	
8.7 ff.	125
8.9	12
9.22	58
10	125
10.4	29
10.19	23
10.19 f.	66
10.20	86
10.25 ff.	125
11.10	126
11.16	108
12.1–3	124
12.14–26	121
13.1	18
15.22	118
15.23 ff.	45
15.24	25 f., 31 f., 42, 116–18
15.24 f.	23
15.24 ff.	29, 46
15.25	31 f., 53, 116
15.25–28	118
15.26	32, 115
15.27	31, 118
15.28	34, 53, 116, 118, 120, 122, 139
15.30 f.	13
II Corinthians	
1.5–7	128
1.8 f.	13
4.3–11	13
6.1	124
6.4 f., 9	13
7.5	13
11.23 ff.	13, 128
Galatians	124
1.8	18
2.20	11
3.19	23, 34
3.22	118
3.23	34
3.23 f.	118
3.23–4.10	123
4.3	23, 45, 118
4.4–7	118
4.8 f.	116
4.9	23, 34, 118
4.11	124
4.14	18
4.26	11
5.1	115, 118

143

Index of Biblical References

Bible Ref.	Page
Galatians—cont.	
5.4	124
5.13	12
5.15	127
Ephesians	52
1.19	117
1.20 f.	42
1.20 ff.	23
1.21	11, 25 f., 32, 45, 117
1.22	31, 117
2.1–6	117
2.2	25 f., 43
2.12	66
2.19	11
3.8–11	117
3.9	118
3.10	25 f., 42, 117
4.1	123
4.18	66
4.22 f.	11
6.5 ff.	12
6.10 ff.	45
6.11 f.	42, 46
6.11 ff.	118
6.12	25 f., 116
6.12 ff.	29
6.17	117, 126
6.18	118
Philippians	
1.23–25	126
1.30	13
2.9	11, 26, 45, 118
2.9 f.	32, 139
2.10	31, 118
2.10 f.	23
3.20	11, 35
3.21	118
Colossians	47, 52, 124
1.15 ff.	36

Bible Ref.	Page
Colossians—cont.	
1.16	25 f., 31, 33, 36, 42, 118 f.
1.16 f.	29, 111, 118
1.17	119
1.20	117 f.
1.21	66
1.24	128
1.26	24
1.26 f.	119
2.6	117
2.6–3.17	123
2.8	45, 116, 118
2.9	36
2.10	22, 25 f., 42, 116, 118 f.
2.12 f.	115
2.15	25–27, 29, 31 f., 42, 45, 116 f., 139
2.20	23, 45, 113, 116, 118
3.1	117
3.1 f.	11
3.1–3	118
3.3, 5 ff.	117
3.22 ff.	12
I Thessalonians	
2.2	13
5	48
II Thessalonians	
2.7	23
I Timothy	
2.1 f.	13
2.1 ff.	39
6.1 f.	12
Titus	
2.9 f.	12
3.1	12 f., 25 f., 42 f., 65

Bible Ref.	Page
Hebrews	
1.2	36
1.3 f.	11
1.4	46
1.5, 7	47
1.10 ff.	36
1.13	46 f.
1.14	33, 46, 60
1–2	22
2.2	23
2.7 f.	118
2.8	53
2.8 f.	126
10.12 f.	118
10.13	31
10.32 f.	13
11.10, 13	11
11.13–16	35
11.26	29
12.2, 22	11
13.14	11, 35
I Peter	
1.1	11, 35
1.14	11
1.17	35
1.20	36
2.11	11
2.13	38
2.13–17	12, 48, 65
2.13 ff.	12 f.
2.16	12
2.17	39
2.18	12
3.22	25 f., 31 f., 42, 45
5.13	12
Revelation	
13	32
13.1	12
13.5	19
13.7	12
17.17	106
21	34

www.ingramcontent.com/pod-product-compliance
Lightning Source LLC
Chambersburg PA
CBHW072154160426
43197CB00012B/2374